DAUGHTER
of the
HEARTLAND

My Ode to the Country That Raised Me

Senator Joni Ernst

Threshold Editions

New York   London   Toronto   Sydney   New Delhi

Threshold Editions
An Imprint of Simon & Schuster, Inc.
1230 Avenue of the Americas
New York, NY 10020

First Threshold Editions hardcover edition May 2020

THRESHOLD EDITIONS and colophon are
trademarks of Simon & Schuster, Inc.

For information about special discounts for bulk purchases,
please contact Simon & Schuster Special Sales at
1-866-506-1949 or business@simonandschuster.com.

The Simon & Schuster Speakers Bureau can bring authors to your live event.
For more information, or to book an event, contact the Simon & Schuster Speakers
Bureau at 1-866-248-3049 or visit our website at www.simonspeakers.com.

Interior design by Jaime Putorti

Manufactured in the United States of America

10   9   8   7   6   5   4   3   2   1

Library of Congress Cataloging-in-Publication Data

Names: Ernst, Joni, 1970– author.
Title: Daughter of the heartland : my ode to the country that raised me /Senator Joni Ernst.
Description: New York : Threshold Editions, 2020. | Summary: "A candid, down-to-earth
    account of Iowa junior senator and veteran Joni Ernst's journey from farm girl to politician,
    and how those values inform her current political career in Washington, DC"—Provided
    by publisher.
Identifiers: LCCN 2020005087 (print) | LCCN 2020005088 (ebook) | ISBN 9781982144869
    (hardcover) | ISBN 9781982144876 (trade paperback) | ISBN 9781982144883 (ebook)
Subjects: LCSH: Ernst, Joni, 1970– | Iowa. General Assembly. Senate—Biography. |
    United States. Congress. Senate—Biography. | Legislators—United States—Biography. |
    Legislators—Iowa—Biography.
Classification: LCC E901.1.E76 A3 2020 (print) | LCC E901.1.E76 (ebook) |
    DDC 328.73/092 [B]—dc23
LC record available at https://lccn.loc.gov/2020005087
LC ebook record available at https://lccn.loc.gov/2020005088

ISBN 978-1-9821-4486-9
ISBN 978-1-9821-4488-3 (ebook)

To Libby, who gives me joy and makes me proud . . .
and to Mom, who has always been there

Contents

FARMER, SOLDIER, MOTHER, SENATOR

I've worn many hats in my lifetime—as a farm girl growing up in a rural community, as a mother raising a daughter who has delighted me and made me proud, as a soldier at home and abroad, and now as a United States senator. But one identity has been the continuous line through everything else I've done—I am an Iowan, a daughter of the heartland.

Iowa is the heartland not just because it's in the center of the country, but also because it's vital to the life of the nation. Mark Twain, who lived for a time in Iowa when he was young, wrote of it in 1863, "the basin of the Mississippi is the BODY OF THE NATION. All the other parts are but members...."

Iowa has always been an aspirational place. First settled thousands of years ago by Native Americans, and part of the great surge west in the 1800s, it became the twenty-ninth state in 1846. By 1854, it was hosting the Iowa State Fair, which remains a signature event to this day. American settlers came to Iowa for the fertile lands and the wide-open spaces, believing that anything was possible away from the congested urban coastline. That sense of promise was in the soil and in the sturdy determination and courage of the people who left the relative security of the East for its unexplored terrain.

Raised in the aspirational heartland, I developed the tenacity that allowed me to pursue my goals. I have my Iowa grounding to thank for my career in the military and state government—and in 2015, I carried my dreams all the way to the United States Senate in Washington, D.C. But I never left Iowa. The genius of our representative government is that Congress is beholden to the local communities. So, everything I do springs from my commitment to serving Iowa and Iowans.

This book is my ode to the heartland I love and the spirit that shaped me. It's the story of the American dream of a farm girl, but more than that, it's an exploration of the values I've lived, and how I've strived to uphold them. I admit that it's a very human story, just one of millions of Americans'. Like most people, I struggle with failures as well as successes—in my marriage, in my ability to get everything I want accomplished. But, with that good old-fashioned Iowa perseverance, I keep moving forward.

We live in a time when media coverage of public officials tends toward the salacious, and we're led to believe that people won't pay attention unless we're screaming at each other. Both sides demonize their opponents and make them into caricatures of evil. It can get exhausting. But I refuse to accept that it's the only way to operate. I learned in the military that you can be tough without being mean, and that the mission requires people to be united in a higher purpose. In the Senate, one of my biggest goals is to cut through the noise and work with everyone who shares my goals—even if they are on the other side of the aisle. Iowans pride ourselves on listening and sharing, which are values that can seem in short supply on the national stage.

As I write this, we are moving into an election season—and a reelection season for me. I know that many political figures write books to coincide with their campaigns. *Daughter of the Heartland* is in part a reflection on my political life, but it is much more than that. Iowans tend to be circumspect in talking about themselves, and that's the way I was raised, too. But I decided it was important at this moment in our history for me to open up and share what it has meant to be a woman winning a place at the table—proving that I can overcome barriers that all women in the military and government encounter. This process has also meant facing some private battles that are painful but necessary to talk about. In politics, we often resist exposing our most personal selves, worrying about showing any sign of weakness. And as women we tend to blame ourselves when we suffer from domestic violence or assault. By telling my story, I hope I can help other women see their troubles in a more empowering light—as well as showing my own daughter the importance of standing up for herself when others try to put her down.

I bring to my narrative strong beliefs about what it means to serve, and how to heal the divisions that afflict our political process. As I pause to think about my life and to consider the coming year, I see 2020 as an inflection point. Running for reelection is a measurably different experience than the first run. In 2014, I was full of ideas and aspirations for Iowa; today, my ideas are enriched by experience. I can evaluate my successes and failures with a clear eye, and lay out my plans for a second term with a confidence hard won over my first term. Serving in the Senate has strengthened my appreciation of who we are as a people, and what we can aspire to be. We can experience crisis, we can fall down and pick ourselves up, we can suffer and cry and move through hardship, but in the end, we are all a part of this wonderful vision of America.

This is the story of my journey, told through the prism of five defining concepts: *home, service, commitment, leadership,* and *grit.* These are the core values that have inspired me, driven me, and supported me during my forty-nine years. They can seem abstract, and they often get stripped of their meaning because we use them so glibly. That's why I decided to wrap them in my experiences—the stories I tell about my life, from the farmlands of Iowa to the halls of Congress.

HOME: For me, home is Iowa, and this book is an ode to the place, but also to the spirit, which transcends a location on the map. Home is a grounding in solid roots, never-changing ideals, and an ancestry that extends back to earlier times. Home is what binds us when the transitory forces of economics, weather, culture, and politics pull us in different directions, when our human institutions crack and falter, and when our futures are hard to see. Home is alive in the ideals that unite us.

SERVICE: During twenty-three years in the military, I found purpose in service. America's armed services are the most fearless, skilled, and driven in the world—and also the most compassionate. As Ronald Reagan once put it, "Democracy is worth dying for, because it's the most deeply honorable form of government ever devised by man." Whether I was serving domestically or in a war zone, I was always conscious of our basic mandate, to protect and improve the lives of others. The ideal of service is generous, kind, and strong in the face of opposition.

COMMITMENT: Public service became a calling for me, a commitment to a larger purpose than myself. It involves politics, of course, but it is not defined by politics. It's really very simple: I am a servant to my constituents, to the Constitution and to the American dream. This commitment means that when I make promises, I work as hard as I can to fulfill them, and when I fail, I get back up and try another way. My constituents don't want excuses, and they can't abide quitters. They want to know that their elected officials won't shift with the political winds.

LEADERSHIP: When I became a U.S. senator, I had to ask myself what kind of senator I was going to be. I strive to be the organizer, the proposer, the one who sees a problem and constructs a legislative solution; the one who constantly reaches out to the other side of the aisle for bipartisan collaborations; the one who can become a role model to young women about what is possible for their futures. Leadership in the Senate often means working out of the spotlight to bring others along on issues I care about.

GRIT: When we face tough situations, we're often told to grit our teeth and endure. But grit is a more profound quality than just enduring. Grit comes from the heart. It's the will to reach beyond disappointment and despair, to face the worst situations of your life and find a way forward. I have experienced crushing personal blows and seemingly insurmountable professional challenges. Grit is the quality—physical, emotional, and spiritual—that always leads me toward the light.

DAUGHTER
of the
HEARTLAND

LISTENING TO IOWA

August 2019

I'm out early on a morning in Iowa, driving with an aide, heading from my home in Red Oak for a full day of events. In the course of the next twelve hours I will travel hundreds of miles, visiting a patchwork of rural towns. As we ride along Highway 34, the sun rises in a red ball over the horizon, painting the fields in shades of gold. It is a serene picture—my favorite time of day. While there is often plenty of truck traffic on these narrow roads, at this hour it's possible to drive for long stretches without seeing many other vehicles, save for the occasional yellow school bus, winding its way between the farms, picking kids up for school.

The landscape is green with the high stalks of corn and the lush blanket of soybeans—the last stage before they brown for harvest in six weeks or so. Along the flat checkerboard of rural roads, the farmhouses glint in the dawn's light, with their sturdy frames, barns, and round, capped silos. It might be a scene from another era, until you look beyond the houses into the fields, where towering wind turbines spin like giant futuristic winged birds, harnessing wind for energy.

For all its hominess and rural ethos, Iowa signals a modern era of technology. People might call us flyover country, and portray us as "hicks in the sticks," but three million Iowans would dispute that. We've all heard the predictions of the decline of rural America, but when you're out in the state what stands out most is the innovation. Iowa leads the nation in wind energy and alternative fuels like ethanol, and our agricultural communities, universities, and businesses have become laboratories for invention. It's not just a matter of progress, but also of survival. Our shrinking labor pool and low unemployment have spurred the development of technologies, including robotics and GPS systems, to help farms function and prosper with fewer hands on the plow. The interest in operational efficiency is an old story on the farms. I remember how relentlessly my dad tinkered with new inventions to make it easier for two people to do the work of three or four.

Many of our farmers have moved to developing precision agriculture, and while it's still basic farming, they've layered technology on top of it, seeking ways to conserve resources and limit the use of chemicals. They're very smart about it and very interested in applying new methods.

That same spirit pervades the Iowa State Fair. People might think the fair is just about who has the biggest hog and the tastiest pork chop on a stick, or which presidential candidate draws the most enthusiastic crowds to the Soapbox. But the real energy of the fair is in ag-tech innovations. The 4-H—such a big influence in my own childhood—and Future Farmers of America clubs are all about industrial expositions that showcase next-generation farming technologies. It's wonderful to see our young people inspired by what they can create.

Today's visits are part of my annual ninety-nine-county tour. I got the idea of visiting all ninety-nine counties every year from Iowa's senior senator, Chuck Grassley. He started doing the tours thirty-nine years ago, and others like me have adopted the practice, which we fondly refer to as "the full Grassley."

Senator Grassley has been my inspiration and my mentor. Few elected officials are as grounded in the heartland as he is. A working farmer himself, his #CornWatch series has delighted Iowans with its practical tutorials on growing and harvesting corn. "Food doesn't grow in supermarkets," he reminds people. "It grows in the fields of rural America by hardworking, dedicated farmers."

I've had people say to me, "Stay in Washington and do your job." They grumble about how often their representatives leave D.C. to go back to their states. Last year I was at a Veterans Day event in Iowa, and I posted a picture of myself with some of the veterans on Facebook. The comments were blistering: "Why aren't you in Washington where we sent you?" And, "I see you're out vacationing on the taxpayer's dollar." But being home is my job, too. I'd hate to imagine what would happen if U.S. senators never left the capital bubble.

Away from the echo chamber I find out what's really going on and achieve a clarity about the issues I could never find a thousand miles away. In Iowa, we share a DNA of being raised on farms, seeing our parents worry through droughts and floods, agonizing over crop yield. We lean in to our manufacturing sectors, too—we're small but competitive. Iowans know what's best for Iowa, and they have some pretty good ideas about what's best for the nation. Their politics are less ideological than practical. I'm always eager to hear them out.

Inside the high school auditorium in Garner in Hancock County— whose motto, "the jewel in the crown of Iowa," is a sign of county pride—people are gathering for a town hall meeting. I hold these meetings regularly. This one will be my eleventh in August, and by the end of my first term, I will have held a town hall in all ninety-nine counties. Often, when I walk into a room, I know many of the attendees by name, and as I make my way to the stage, I try engaging as many people as I can.

Town halls are unpredictable and sometimes contentious. I've heard my share of boos. The media likes to play up the outbursts and the arguments, treating town halls as a form of blood sport. I've noticed that my town halls only get headlines if there's a colorful confrontation, where people in the audience shout and wave opposition signs. The gleeful report—"Ernst confronted at town hall meeting"—will be the first item on a Google search of my name for a few weeks.

I have to be honest, it bugs me sometimes when people go on the attack. A better way to get my attention is to engage me in a conversation, even if our views differ.

For the most part, town meetings are bread-and-butter events—a chance for my constituents to share their concerns and for me to tell them what's going on in Washington and how I'm representing their interests in the Senate and with the president.

In my experience, most people come to town halls because they care about issues. Not abstractions, but issues that directly affect them. Sometimes it seems as if we're living in two national realities—one involving media obsessions and another involving real-world concerns. What I know about Iowans is that they're very discerning. They've heard it all from politicians, and they recognize nonsense when they hear it. They've seen the parade of outsiders come in trying to woo their votes during every presidential election season, and they see right through the empty promises. They live in the here and now. And if you're going to represent them, you'd better understand them—something presidential candidates who roll down rural roads in their big campaign buses don't always get.

Back in 2008, after candidate Barack Obama won the Iowa caucus, he followed up his win by calling rural communities like ours "bitter," and saying we "cling to guns or religion." He said this in a private gathering, but it leaked out, letting us know how he really felt. This contempt for our lives is something we're used to hearing from outsiders, and we resent it. When I'm out in the state, I don't see bitter people. I see Americans who have the same dreams and struggles as everyone else. Our principles are formed in the soil; our pride is in what we can grow and make. Our victories are hard won and appreciated all the more.

Simply put, we Iowans care even more about what's going on in our farmlands and in our communities than what's happening on the national stage. Moms worry about putting food on the table and buying football cleats for their kids and new clothes for school. Washington, on the other hand, is very caught up in itself. It tends to forget what it's like to listen to the people it's trying to help. We all need a regular dose of town hall meetings to bring us back to earth.

Hyperpartisanship has infected our dialogue these days, and that's a shame. Iowa has never been defined by parties, and although it leans conservative, it can also be a swing state. My predecessor was a Democrat, Tom Harkin, who served for thirty years. We've never been people who couldn't talk to each other, but I see it happening now more than ever, and I do what I can in Washington to break that impasse. I always keep in mind that when I was in the National Guard helping flood-ravaged communities at home, or overseas trucking urgently needed supplies from Kuwait into Iraq, nobody ever stopped to ask what party I belonged to. We shared common missions then. Why can't we do some of that in our politics?

It's no secret that there's a lot of pressure to stay loyal to our parties. Agreeing with the other side on any bill means being called a traitor by some. In that sense, being a senator sometimes feels harder for me than being in the military, where we always put country above all other considerations. Everyone's constantly spinning things their way. There's no right or wrong. Just your party and its stances. But what happens when party lines interfere with the country's needs?

On one occasion in 2018, I was leaving an event, when a middle-aged man and his son came up to me in the parking lot.

"Why are you doing a bill with Elizabeth Warren?" he demanded, outraged. He was talking about the bill we had introduced for veterans to improve research on traumatic brain injury. As a vet it was close to my heart.

"I'm glad to work with Senator Warren on a bill that's so important to veterans," I told him. Then I walked off and left him standing there in the parking lot with his mouth opening and closing like a guppy, his son next to him mortified.

Iowans are especially knowledgeable about national issues because they have a big voice in presidential elections. The status of our state as a first caucus setting raises educated voters. There are few other places in the nation where ordinary folks can claim to have had in-depth personal conversations with multiple presidential candidates. My constituents sometimes express annoyance at being bombarded by phone calls, emails, and campaign ads, but overall they're proud of the distinction as a caucus first, and they enjoy the process, regardless of the candidates. It's important for them to know they have access.

On a day-to-day basis, it also means they have high expectations of their representatives, and that's okay with me. I wasn't sent to Washington to be a potted plant.

At this town meeting in the small community of Garner, people are worried about two main issues: the impact of tariffs and barriers to ethanol production. Perched on a high stool, a table next to me so I can take notes, I focus on these issues and tell them straight out how disappointed I am with the Environmental Protection Agency's harmful decision, announced in early August, to offer exemptions from the biofuel law to 31 of 37 oil refineries in the United States. These refineries would not be required to blend ethanol with gasoline, as the law stipulates. That's a big deal, and it's already having a negative effect on the ethanol production that Iowa depends on. Iowa's main crops are the corn and soybeans used to make biofuels. The EPA's decision is particularly upsetting because President Trump came to Council Bluffs, Iowa, on June 11 and promised to support ethanol. Folks out here understand that the ethanol exemptions literally put Iowa's economy at stake. I agree, telling them, "It's a slap at farmers. It really sets us back quite a bit." The maddening thing about it is that the goal of exemptions is to prevent small oil refineries from going out of business. But some of these so-called small refineries are actually owned by Chevron and Exxon.

I tell the worried attendees about my conversations with the president. Basically, I've sought to educate him, as has Senator Grassley and our former governor Terry Branstad, who is now the U.S. ambassador to China. This is deeply serious business that could harm Trump's standing with Iowa voters—and a couple of people at this town meeting say as much. The thing is, they *want* to support the president. In my view, it's an unforced error on the part of the administration, made by the EPA without fully appreciating the effect it would have.

It's just one more burden for farmers who are suffering as a result of tariffs. Once again, the people in this room do support the president. But it's hard to stomach the falling prices, and believe me, the bailout money doesn't feel like an answer to hardworking farmers. "I'll take the money. I appreciate the money," one young farmer says. "But I want to sell in the market, not receive a payment from the government." It's a sentiment I hear over and over again. Another gentleman says sadly that he's had to find work elsewhere. He just can't make it.

An older farmer rises slowly to his feet and says, "I might lose my farm, but we have to be patriotic. If it means sticking it to the Chinese, we should support the policy."

Another farmer acknowledges, "Yeah, this really sucks. We're going to have to rethink our strategy moving forward. And maybe we don't get the new equipment we had wanted to get this year, but the president is doing the right thing with trade."

This feeling is one reason Iowa farmers haven't rebelled against the president. They're hoping for long-term rewards, and they don't trust the Chinese. Neither do I. But the fear of economic suffering is well-founded. The president and I speak often, and I appreciate his willingness to listen and hear from me. On this issue though, he expresses his deep conviction about tariffs, adding, "I know you don't like tariffs, Joni."

It's true. Trade agreements are essential to my constituents. We began the year worried about Chinese retaliation, but also frustrated that the United States–Mexico–Canada Agreement (USMCA), a modernized trade deal that was announced in 2018, had yet to be ratified. (Much to my relief, the USMCA would be finished in February 2020—a true credit to the president, who worked hard to get a deal done. He also finalized a phase-one China deal. I wasn't under any illusions that this deal would solve all of our issues with China, but it was a step forward, and one that came with significant agricultural purchases that would benefit Iowa farmers.)

After the town meeting, I hang around to speak with folks informally. They want to shake my hand, look me in the eye, and tell me to fight for them back in Washington. A middle-aged man comes up to me and says, "I'm a farmer who isn't farming anymore. It's gone. So now I'm working at a diner. I take what work I can get. Someone else has my farm now, and we're renting a place in town." The pain is indescribable, because it's not just this man's lifelong work that's gone; it's his family's legacy. It's his identity.

I see the familiar heartbreak in his face that I've known all my life through the hard times of farming—when my parents struggled or when neighbors came by to tearfully announce they were losing their farms. But now I have a responsibility to help shape policies that will protect them. I promise the people gathered around me, "Every day I wake up in the morning fighting for you."

Back on the road, I carry with me those worried faces as I make the hour-and-a-half drive to my next event. Sometimes what they don't say is just as poignant as what they do say. Iowans are famously stoic, and farmers most of all. Sometimes I think that maybe Americans would understand farmers better and rally to them more if they heard their pain. But it's not easy to get them to talk about it. My job is to bring their voices to the nation, and that means sharing with my fellow senators and the president what life is like in rural communities, because if you don't experience it, sometimes it's hard to see.

There's a lot of windshield time doing the ninety-nine-county tour. We try to cluster the counties together. But sometimes I have to go out of my way when I'm asked to be a guest speaker or attend a special event. I'm used to all the driving, as many Iowans are. In the rural areas, you don't just "run out" to pick up household items, school supplies, gardening tools, or a new pair of gloves. Many of the big stores are gone. When I was a kid, people stayed closer to home. There were stores all around the square and on Broadway in Red Oak—a Pamida department store and a Kmart, and when Pamida closed it was replaced by ShopKo. But now that's changed, with Kmart closing in 2018 and ShopKo in 2019. All that's left for basic household items is the Family Dollar or Dollar General stores. The nearest Walmart is twenty-five miles away in Shenandoah. So, it's a long drive for the simplest purchases, and if you need something more substantial, like a laptop or desktop computer, or dishwasher, it can be an hour or more. Looking at it on the brighter side, I like to think these distances don't separate us but bring us closer to our fellow Iowans. I figure, you can live in a city and never leave it because everything is there at your disposal. But out in the rural areas you're exposed to many different communities just in the course of living your life. Still, we really miss our Kmart.

As the sun sets I head back toward Red Oak. I'll be spending the evening in Stanton, the community eight miles to the southeast where I was raised and where my father and uncle still live on their farms and my brother, Wade, lives with his family. My brother doesn't farm. He works for the railroad now as a heavy equipment operator. He started farming right out of high school and it just wasn't what he wanted to do. But he still lives in our old area. My sister Julie is the only one of the three of us who still farms.

When I make the turn toward Stanton, I am alone on the deserted road. There isn't a house in sight. But sitting nestled behind a small gas station at the side of the road is the Stanton Child Resource Center, a little day care center that means a lot to me. I see it as an important symbol of a reality about rural communities. Some people call us child care deserts. The Stanton center is the only nonprofit day care for many miles around—it actually serves several counties.

There's a huge waiting list at the Stanton Center, and funds are always a struggle. We're not a wealthy community, and the center has exhausted nearly all the funding programs available. Since I serve on the Small Business Administration committee, I wanted to do something to address this need, which is widespread in rural America. So, in 2019 I reached across the aisle to my Democratic colleague

Jacky Rosen of Nevada, and we collaborated on a bill that would allow nonprofit child care providers to utilize programs offered by the Small Business Administration. It might seem like a very small thing, but rural communities need child care just as urgently as cities and suburbs.

My longtime friend Sheila Mainquist is involved with the center, and when I told her about the bill she was overjoyed. "How soon will the bill be done?" she asked eagerly.

"Oh, Sheila," I said apologetically. "We've just introduced it and things don't happen overnight." That's the frustrating fact about legislation, but at least we'd started the process moving.

I pull into Wade's driveway and see that the "Chicken Coop" is lit up. Wade's Chicken Coop has become a local gathering place for friends and family. It's an example of the way Iowans out in these rural areas get together. We don't have many town watering holes, so people organize impromptu socials in barns and outbuildings.

The Coop is a spacious shack behind Wade's house, which he's designed to the hilt with his special brand of cozy. There are tables, stools, a serving counter, a cooking stove, and even a toilet. Wade's unique style is on display in rugged, personalized décor and signs. It's big enough to fit forty people. Wade is a charming guy and a natural host—his annual Halloween party (costume required) is a favorite event. Dogs and cats and sometimes rabbits wander through the Coop at will.

Tonight is just a chance to hang out with old friends and enjoy the last days of summer. Everybody brings a dish or plugs in a Crock-Pot. Most of the neighbor kids we grew up with are still around. Some have taken over family farm operations. We don't talk much about politics. Mostly we catch up on how our kids and parents are doing, gossip about people we know, and reminisce. There's lots of easygoing laughter. I meet many people in my work, and I've made some lasting friends in my public service—both in the Army and National Guard and in public life. But there's nothing quite like being with those who really *know* you from the time you were a gap-toothed farm kid. I always have the same warm sensation: it's good to be home. In Iowa I am surrounded by the power of community.

Tomorrow I'll be back on the road. This summer "break" is a chance for me to store up images and input, the way a silo stores grain, ready to take them back with me to Capitol Hill, where the voices of the people can sometimes seem very far away.

HOME

Home is the place you put down your stake, but it's also a relationship to others and the world. People often talk about the quality Iowans have called "Iowa nice." It's real, and it's not saccharine. It's a spirit of community—of doing for others. Every Sunday when I was a child, we'd gather in the sanctuary of our church, sitting on wooden pews. We'd sing the old Lutheran hymns, and then our pastor got up behind the pulpit and talked about God's love and how we ought to treat each other. We took him at his word. We were a strong community, even outside of Sunday mornings. If someone had a family member who was sick, the community showed up with cakes and breads and casseroles to put in the freezer. If someone was going through a rough patch, the community banded together and prayed. A lot has changed in our world, but that sense of community is one thing that's stayed the same. It's what I think about when I think of home.

In Washington D.C., we all come from someplace else. That's what representative government in the United States is all about. We come together to make decisions for the country, but we are grounded by our ties to home. Iowa is a special place to call home in that regard. There is a reason why presidential candidates come to Iowa every four years to launch their primary season with our caucuses. If you were to ask for a definition of the heartland, it would be Iowa. When I fly home from Washington, I always feel as if I can take a deep breath again when I get off the plane. I want to introduce you to my home because I believe it holds an important lesson for all of us about America's greatness.

Chapter One

FARM GIRL

One of my earliest childhood memories is sitting next to my dad in the big cab of our combine, my small legs dangling over the seat, rolling through the cornfield at harvest time. Through the glass window I could see the world go by, the puffy clouds, the occasional flight of a hawk, as the rows of cornstalks were smoothly pulled up and pushed into the auger. This was my way of "helping," but it was very peaceful, and after a while the slow, steady motion would lull me to sleep until we had a full load.

When I was older, I got to drive a tractor myself, hauling a corn-filled wagon to the bins. I was proud to be given this responsibility, although I wasn't very good at backing up the wagon. Fortunately, it wasn't possible to do much damage out in the open field.

I always loved working out in the fields with their endless rows of corn and soybeans and the sky above so big and clear. Harvesting wasn't mentally taxing—you could daydream in the fields.

This was our farm, north of Stanton, Iowa, and it had been my grandfather's farm before us. My father, Dick Culver's family had a long history in the area. My father's family came up in the Hastings-Tabor area of Mills County—one county over from where they would eventually make a life in Montgomery County.

My paternal grandfather was a farmer, but during World War II he had a different role, as many people did. He worked for the airplane manufacturer Glenn L. Martin Company at Offutt Air Force Base near Omaha, Nebraska, close to the Iowa border. His job was to do modifications on the *Enola Gay*, the aircraft that dropped the first atom bomb on Hiroshima.

It was a top-secret mission, of course. He used to say that the modifications were done in the middle of the country to avoid the threat of spies, who were less likely to find their way to the farmlands. He was a supervisor, and he'd only receive one set of blueprints at a time, to contain access to this vital information. And they would only bring the plane out of the hangar at night, after dark.

After that mission, my grandfather was sent to California for a while, along with my grandmother, who worked as a seamstress for a wealthy woman. After the war, they returned to Iowa and farmed their land in Montgomery County, which would eventually become my family's home.

My mother, Marilyn's family came from Page and Taylor Counties, in the southwest corner of the state. They were farmers, but my mother's father was killed in a car accident before my mother was born. So my grandmother, who had two children already and was expecting my mom, moved back in with her father, and he helped them get by. Eventually my grandmother met and married the man who I knew as my grandfather, a sweet man who was a farmhand, welder, and church janitor. They settled in Red Oak, and my grandmother got a job at the Eveready battery plant, working on the line. They were very poor, but they got by with my grandmother's homespun skills—she sewed their clothes, grew vegetables and fruit, and canned food for the winter. Those skills were passed down to my mother and then to my sister and me.

One of my fondest recollections is of the time we spent canning with my grandmothers, great-aunts, aunts, and cousins. It was a family event. We'd can beets, pickles, tomatoes, sweet corn, and green beans, and make jam. I learned that you could can just about anything. In our basement, shelves were filled with jars of vegetables, which saw us through the winter months. In time, supermarket canned goods became so cheap that we really didn't need to do it anymore, but we continued the tradition because we valued the time together so much—and in our opinion, home-canned vegetables beat the supermarket brands every time.

Now, when I think about my grandmothers and great-aunts, I visualize them in our farm kitchen, laughing and talking as they taught my sister and me and my cousins how to do it right.

These visceral memories are the artifacts of my childhood. People then didn't talk that much about what they'd experienced or how they'd suffered. We didn't hear long, drawn-out stories about their lives—the way you might hear today. Whenever I tried to probe, I'd get the same smiles and shrugs, and only the smallest unsatisfactory doses of information. It wasn't that people didn't *remember* their pasts. It's just that they had learned to hold it all in, to protect themselves. It was a form of Iowa dispassion. I never recall my grandmothers or aunts really talking about their hardships, and my parents were the same way. In Iowa, you endured and moved on.

But the baking sessions I *do* remember. As an adult, when I lived in a house with apple and pear trees, I made applesauce and canned pears, and I taught my daughter to do it. My mother doesn't live on a farm anymore, but she'll still can. It's not a necessity, but it provides a sense of self-esteem and a bit of nostalgia.

My parents met in high school in Red Oak, and were married soon after my mother finished beauty school and moved to the farm north of Stanton. My sister Julie was born in 1969, and I came along on July 1, 1970, the middle child of three. The local radio station announced my birth, which was the custom at the time. It's the way neighbors found out key life events in an era before Facebook and Instagram.

My brother, Wade, was born six years later, and everyone in the family was pretty excited to have a boy at last. My father's brother Dallas had five girls, so Wade was the only boy of eight grandchildren. We used to complain that he got away with everything, though I don't think he remembers it that way.

We all loved each other in the way only a family can, even though we didn't say the words "I love you" often. Part of how I expressed love for my sister was defending her when she was bullied in school. Julie was diagnosed with juvenile diabetes—as was Wade—and she was teased about it constantly. She had a really tough time with the other kids growing up. I suffered right along with her. A jab at her was like a jab at me. Decades later, she would return the fierce protection when I was struggling in my marriage. Even though Julie and I were close, we were nothing alike. She was a tomboy, and I dressed on the girly side. She welded, I sewed. The list goes on. But we stood up for each other.

Growing up, we didn't have much. It was a typical farming family's life. We did chores: fed the hogs, shoveled manure, and participated fully in other forms of manual labor. We worked hard, as all farm children do, but it was the best childhood a country girl could ask for. It was simple and idyllic—dirt roads and small-town America. The idea that there is strength in numbers proved itself time and again, on and off the farm. We relied on each other for the hard work that needed doing, and we got it done. There was no place in our household for anyone to be a prima donna.

Our farm was in Montgomery County, which is a place with a deep history. It was first settled by Native Americans more than ten thousand years ago, and artifacts are still uncovered every year.

When white settlers arrived in the 1800s, they put down stakes near a stream surrounded by oaks. To this day, Red Oak is the heart of the county. It's a beautiful place, with charming, tree-lined streets and old Victorian homes built for wealthy residents of the nineteenth century. Red Oak has a thriving downtown, a world-class health center, and miles of hiking trails and parkland.

A short distance away, Stanton is a small town that was settled by Swedish immigrants and still has a strong Swedish culture. It's barely a blip on the radar, with fewer than 700 residents—a number that hasn't changed much since I was a kid. We went to elementary school at the Stanton Community School, which has since been converted to the Swedish Heritage and Cultural Center. Visiting the center is nostalgic for me. They still have some of the old wooden desks I remember so well.

For a long time, the signature of Stanton was a giant Swedish coffeepot set atop the water tower, which could be seen for miles around. People would use it for directions—"one mile north of the coffeepot"..."two blocks east of the coffeepot." The coffeepot was placed on the tower as part of the 1970 centennial celebration, and it was a nod to Stanton's most famous native—Virginia Christine, popularly known as Mrs. Olsen of the Folger's coffee commercials. The coffeepot eventually fell into disrepair and was removed to the museum in 2015. It was a sad day for Stanton residents.

The main church in Stanton is the Mamrelund Lutheran Church, where Mom and I still go. The high point of every year was—and still is—the Santa Lucia festival in December, which brings the whole community together to celebrate this symbol of Swedish history and culture. As children, we looked forward to the festival. It's a commemoration of Saint Lucia, a fourth-century martyr who lit her way in the catacombs by tying a burning torch to her head. But you don't have to be religious or Swedish to get involved. In addition to the religious connotation, it marks the beginning of winter, and symbol-izes lighting the way during the dark days. The community ceremony involves electing one girl to be Saint Lucia and walk with a lit wreath of candles on her head (they use battery-operated lights these days), preceded by other girls, all dressed in white. The lucky girl is chosen by a public vote, and it is considered a tremendous honor. I was never chosen, but my daughter Libby did have the honor one year.

Dad wasn't much of a churchgoer, but Mom took us kids to church and Sunday school every week. For some reason, which no one can explain, we weren't baptized until I was twelve. I think life just got busy around the farm, and finally one day Mom announced, "Let's get everyone baptized"—and that included Dad, too. I was always involved in the church and taught Sunday school as a teen-ager.

Having faith is important, but I admit I didn't really appreciate it until I got older. Then, I saw the way it helped me get through so many difficult experiences. I really felt the importance of faith when I was in the National Guard and deployed to the Middle East. When things seemed impossible, my faith—always rooted in my family and Iowa—reminded me to trust in God and realize that some things were out of my hands.

Life on a farm was a constant battle for survival. We grew soy-beans and corn, as most of the farmers in our area did. There's a little more diversity in crops in central and eastern Iowa—such as melon and pumpkins and large cattle ranches. But most of the corn and soybeans we harvested were rolled into the feedstock for livestock, and much of that feedstock was exported to other countries.

In my childhood, nearly every farm had livestock. We had hogs on our farm. I was ten years old the first time I castrated a hog. I was doing my usual chores one afternoon when Dad rounded up my sister, Julie, and me. "Come out to the barn with me, girls," he said, and we dropped what we were doing to follow him outside, not suspecting what was in store—a lesson in hog castration. Inside the barn were the young hogs, and in a matter-of-fact, clinical way Dad demonstrated how to hold the scalpel and where to grab the pig so that we could make the incision into the scrotal sac with surgical accuracy, and then pull the testicles out. He talked us through the steps, and my stomach lurched at the sight of what was happening in front of me. I didn't know that it would be my turn next until Dad handed me the scalpel. I was a mess of nerves that first time. I'll never forget the smell of blood and the choking cloud of dust the hog kicked up into my face. I'll never forget the slimy feel of the testicles as I reached in and yanked them out. And most of all, I'll never forget the squeals. (I'd later use this experience in my run for the Senate. It was the core message of my 2014 Make 'em Squeal campaign. More about that later.)

Castrating hogs is one of those jobs nobody wants to do, but it has to be done, and it's disgusting. It was a family affair involving Dad, Mom, Julie, and me. Wade, being too small to cut, would trail behind us with a spray bottle of iodine to give the pigs a squirt on the incision to prevent infection. We had a bucket and we'd save the decent-sized testicles for frying. The delicacy, known as mountain oysters, is dense and chewy. I never liked them—maybe I was too close to the retrieval process—but mountain oysters are very popular. The smaller or damaged testicles would get tossed, usually right onto the barn floor, where the pigs would eat them.

The circle of life is very real on the farm. We'd make pets out of the cute little piglets, and we'd play with them and love them. But we knew at some point they were going to go away. We participated in that process, too. Dad would announce that it was time to sort the hogs, picking out the bigger hogs that were ready for market. We'd chase them around the hog lot, trying to sort them by size. There's a special way to pick up a hog once you catch it. If you try to pick it up by wrapping your arms around its midsection, it will squeal like crazy. The mama sows will get very agitated if they hear their piglets squealing and things will get ugly fast. So, we'd pick them up by the hind legs and carry them to the barn, where Dad was waiting. When the hogs were ready to be sold, the hog buyer would arrive and load them into his trailer. Off our little piggies would go to market. From an early age, we learned that this was part of life, and although we were momentarily sad, we understood.

I know pigs are considered to be intelligent creatures. I've read all the studies on pig cognition. But as a child, I didn't need studies to tell me that our beloved farm animals were smart and sensitive—I could see it in their big warm eyes and by how quickly the little ones caught on to routines. My siblings and I loved them, but we were also taught that these wonderful animals were part of the life cycle of the farm.

Dad didn't let Julie and me show hogs at the county fair, because he thought it was too much work, but I had friends who did. They'd raise their prize animals and be filled with pride to show them at the fair. But after that, the hogs, which were practically domesticated, would be sold for slaughter. Tough lessons! There were lots of tears at the end of the fair when the beloved animals were carted away.

One year my sister Julie chose to raise a steer as part of a Future Farmers of America project. She brought the steer home and we named him Buck. He was the sweetest thing. He'd follow Julie around the farm as if he were a puppy. She didn't even need a harness.

Buck was so well-behaved that one day when Mom wasn't home, we let him come into our living room. Thinking back, it was an incredibly stupid thing to do. Buck could have trashed the place in seconds! Lucky for us, Buck behaved, and Mom never found out about it until recently when I confessed.

At the end of the semester, Julie was graded on Buck's growth, and then Dad took him down to the meat locker in Stanton, where he was butchered. Buck went into the freezer, and none of us had a problem eating him, although we cried when we said good-bye. It's just the way life was on the farm.

Mom's job was to cook for my dad and uncle and the others who were working in the fields. Harvesting was always a community affair, with the farmers helping each other. They'd move from field to field, and eat their meals at each homestead. We didn't have cattle, but everyone would pitch in to help the farmers who did. This was true of all farm activities. Haying would also take everyone's efforts, and the farmers would help each other sort cattle or hogs, plant crops, and bring in the harvest.

During the busiest times, Dad and Mom didn't leave the farm much, and we had our chores after school—cooking meals, growing vegetables in the garden, and hosing down the hogs (because they don't sweat). I don't remember anyone complaining, but Mom later mentioned that she sometimes felt tied down. When she was cooking for the men, it would take all morning, and then she'd clean up, fix lunch, and take it out to the field, before she turned around to do it all again. She didn't have an outside life, except for occasional visits to a neighbor's farm for coffee, or her Stitch and Chatter Club. So, although farming often involved the community, it could also be isolating. This was especially true in the winters. Winters were devoted to post-harvest and pre-planting maintenance and repairs. After Dad's morning coffee, he would bundle up in his coveralls and head out to the machine shed, where he would clean or repair the farm equipment in anticipation of spring. There were still a multitude of chores, just different chores depending on the season.

The winters were often brutal, and the upstairs of our little farmhouse where we slept as kids could get very cold. Julie and I would wake up to frost on our bedroom windows—on the inside. We'd scratch smiley faces in the frost, then head downstairs wrapped in our blankets to the kitchen, where it was guaranteed to be warm. We would huddle over the heat registers while Mom made breakfast—sausage or bacon with fried eggs and toast. The house was heated by a wood-burning furnace in the basement. It was our job to carry the split wood from the woodshed to the giant box in the basement to feed the furnace. Trip after trip through the snow, one armload at a time.

When winter rolled in, so did the hunting seasons. Many neighbors would take advantage of the deer seasons for additional meat to add into the mix of farm-raised poultry, pork, or beef. I didn't participate in pheasant or deer hunting as a young girl, but we kids would shoot clay pigeons tossed with a handheld thrower off the terrace with Dad's shotgun and shoot at cans with an old .22 rifle. It wasn't a competitive exercise between us. Instead it was a time of bonding and encouragement, and we took great delight in shattering the clays with the quick but steady pull of the trigger.

Mom was a doer. She became the leader of our 4-H club, which was an important source of socialization and learning. Our efforts were devoted to creating products to take to the county fair. We'd sew and embroider and grow vegetables and make preserves. We'd can vegetables, refinish furniture, do woodworking, and create photographic exhibits. We were always busy. And we were all procrastinators. We'd wait until the last few weeks before fair to try to get a project done. Mom was always there trying to push us along.

Looking back, I realize how grateful I am for 4-H. It taught me lessons in self-sufficiency, and also helped me develop confidence. I was quiet and shy, very much an introvert when I was younger. Interacting with other kids on 4-H projects helped bring me out of my shell. It was also lighthearted, a release from what were the very real struggles of making ends meet on the farm.

Our household was run in a frugal way, but we got by. For example, we each had one pair of good shoes. Mom used to keep a drawer full of empty bread bags, and when it rained, we would slip our feet into the bread bag–covered shoes, and that would keep our shoes clean and dry while we were waiting for the school bus or going to church. Everybody did that then. It just showed we were thrifty—when you only had one pair of good shoes, you protected those shoes.

Our parents mostly tried to insulate us from the economic struggles on the farm. The 1980s were particularly tough years. I can remember the worry, and also my mom saying, "Joni, we'll figure out a way to get through this. We'll make it happen. Together."

But Dad and Mom had to find outside sources of income when the farm economy began to tank. Dad had a side construction business, starting with one bulldozer, doing terracing and other dirt-work jobs. As soon as Wade was in school, Mom took a part-time job down at the sale barn in Stanton, where she worked the cattle auctions. She also did a stint as secretary at our church. Eventually she got a job at Belt GM Chevy, a car dealer, and then at the courthouse, working for the county treasurer in the motor vehicles office in Red Oak. So, she worked hard off the farm, too. I don't think we fully appreciated that as kids. Families did what they had to do.

In the face of hardship, the community came together. There were no questions asked. We believed that every farmer's struggle belonged to all of us, and we pitched in. If a farmer was injured and couldn't take care of his harvest or livestock, a call would go out on the radio, notifying the community that help was needed, and the community would show up with combines and tractors and wagons to harvest his corn or take care of his animals. They'd tell his family,

"Don't worry. We've got this." The response is second nature in farm communities, and it still is today.

Weather was a constant worry, and a force outside our control. A few days of rain at the wrong time could undermine the entire harvesting operation. So could drought. You couldn't harvest beans that were too dry because the pods would crack open and spill the beans onto the ground. Tornadoes would pull the corn out of the ground or lay it flat, making it impossible for combines to grab the stalks. Bug infestations could demolish crops. I remember a particularly bad beetle infestation one year, and beetles continue to be a threat. Farmers can try to control it by crop dusting, but that costs money.

I can recall times when there were terrible floods in Iowa, and once again, the call would go out. People would travel from across the state, bringing supplies and helping with cleanup. If a store got flooded, volunteers would show up to scoop out mud. I know this happens in other places during disasters, but in farm communities it's second nature.

I was a quiet kid, a bookworm. I loved to read. Trixie Belden books—adventure stories about a brave girl—were my favorite. (I still own twenty-six books from the series.) We have the wonderful Carnegie Library in Red Oak. Built in 1909, it's a historic site that was remodeled fifteen years ago. Whenever Mom brought us to town, we'd head straight for the library. We also had a little bookstore on the town square, and once I started earning a little money from babysitting, I could buy my own books. Sadly, that bookstore is long gone.

I was a very bright student, and a bit of a teacher's pet. My fourth-grade teacher, Mrs. Sundberg, was my greatest advocate. I still remember the impression she made on me. When I took the Iowa Basic Skills Test, she rushed to tell me that I scored in the

95–99 percentage range for all Iowa students, and she was jumping up and down, hugging me. All my teachers were cheerleaders for their kids. We were lucky in that way.

But then I started to have problems. My seat in Mrs. Sundberg's classroom was in the back of the room, and one day she pulled me aside to talk to me about my math homework. She had written the problems on the board and we'd copied them down to do the answers at home. Every one of my problems was wrong, and Mrs. Sundberg was baffled. "Your answers are right, but these aren't the problems that were on the board," she said. I felt devastated. I couldn't understand how it had happened. But Mrs. Sundberg figured it out. She contacted my parents and suggested they get my eyes tested. Once I started wearing glasses, everything became clear. I hadn't realized what I was missing. I didn't love being the girl with the Coke-bottle eyeglasses—the frames were so big they covered half my face—but at least I could see again.

I could spend hours curled up with a book, but I also loved being outdoors. I participated in every sport available—volleyball, softball, cheerleading—and my diaries from those years are filled with schedules for sporting events and school activities. No one would have considered me a jock. I was more an athletic bookworm.

With the grand landscape of our childhood, we kids spent a lot of time outdoors. When we weren't doing farm chores, we were running in groups, cutting through the cornfields, and fishing crawdads out of the tree-lined creek below our property. There were a lot of kids at neighboring farms then, something you don't see as much of anymore. Many of those households are gone, and kids today don't have as many neighbors to play with. I am thankful, though, that my nephews play in that same creek today.

By the time we were in sixth grade, we all had motorcycles—dirt bikes, really—and we'd pick up our friends and go riding, exploring the trails and fields in our wide-open world. Dad had a motorcycle, too. When he was out in the field and needed something from the shop, it was convenient for him to hop on his bike and go.

We had an old Glastron boat stored in the barn. Every year we'd haul it down to the state park in Adams County in Dad's old blue Ford pickup, bringing neighbor kids along. The kids rode in back on a mattress under the topper, bouncing with every bump Dad hit along the way. Then we'd arrive, unpack the gear, and go water skiing. We went so often that I was slaloming by the time I was in sixth grade. I had the time of my life out on the water with my family in that old boat. To this day, I smile when I think about it.

With all the fun, farms were also places of constant danger. When we were little kids we were lectured about the things that could happen to us if we weren't careful. Out in the yard, Mom watched us like a hawk, but Julie was a particularly daring toddler—she'd be out of the house and into the barn before anyone knew she was gone. She'd head for the pens where the hogs were kept, and even after my folks built a wire fence, she could wriggle under it. It used to give my parents heartburn. Eventually they put a fence around the yard to corral us.

We all heard the horror stories of farmers getting trapped in grain bins and suffocating, and horrible injuries with augers that could rip an arm off, or tractors that rolled over on inclines crushing the driver. Once, a high school boy helping to hay at a nearby farm got knocked off a trailer barge onto the gravel, and that messed him up pretty bad. Another time, a farmer was pushed up against a fence by a cow and was injured so badly he passed away. It was a freak accident. The whole community showed up to bring in the harvest for his wife.

Rules were drummed into us about what we could do and what we could *never* do. We were taught to respect the equipment, the animals, and nature.

*   *   *

When I dreamed about my life, I never saw myself leaving Iowa. In a second-grade project, we were asked what we wanted to be when we grew up, and with the confidence of a seven-year-old, I wrote:

Nurse

Farmer's wife

Miss America

Of course, Miss America never came to pass, but I was quite serious about being a nurse. One Christmas, Mom sewed me a little nurse's uniform, complete with a red cross attached with a safety pin. I wore it all the time. I never became a nurse, although I did major in psychology and spent two years volunteering at a women's crisis shelter.

As for being a farmer's wife, it just seemed inevitable when I was young. When you grow up in a small rural community, you only know what you know. I admired my mother and my grandmother. It didn't feel like such a stretch that I would grow up to be like them. Maybe that's where the nurse idea came from, too. Since both my siblings had juvenile diabetes, Mom was the one who gave them their shots and made sure they ate the right diet.

When we were children, my parents had a solid relationship, but it wasn't all domestic bliss on the farm. There were hard times, and now when I look at it I realize that there was some depression. Depression is actually quite common for farmers, especially when there are financial troubles, or burnout from the pressing workload. Nobody ever talked about it when I was growing up, but today we're more aware. In 2018, my Democratic colleague Tammy Baldwin and

I cosponsored a bill to include mental health services for farmers in the farm bill. This bipartisan effort acknowledged the difficulty of farming and how it can lead to depression. A big part of the problem is that farmers are used to being self-sufficient and stoic about their troubles. They have pride. They're not always comfortable reaching out. They're more accustomed to being the ones who provide support to others. But we were shocked to learn when we were working on the bill that, according to the Centers for Disease Control and Prevention, the suicide rate among farmers was shockingly high.

When I was a kid, there were occasional suicides in our community. A farmer's wife hung herself in a barn, and another neighbor shot himself in despair after the bank refused to loan him money. We were shocked, but at the time we just considered them unusual tragedies. It was never a matter of reevaluating mental health among farmers.

When I was in my late twenties, I watched my parents go through their own hardship, and they grew apart. With the kids out of the house, Dad became restless. He enjoyed going out with friends and having a beer or two, while Mom preferred to stay home. The bonds of their marriage frayed. They eventually divorced, and Mom moved to a house in Red Oak. It was very hard for all of us. The ups and downs of farm life can take their toll on the best of families. Depression, alcoholism, and other societal issues affect good people, even in the heartland.

Julie, Wade, and I are sad that our parents are no longer together, because in many ways it was the end of an era for us—the broken dream of a farm family.

I find myself reminiscing about the great childhood we had out in the fields, feeling the wind in our faces and being so free and alive. Those are happy recollections, even when there were little calamities—like the time I face-planted in a gardener spiderweb (those spiders were huge!). Or the time Wade got stuck in the hog wallow and I pulled him right out of his boots straight into the muck—barefoot. We laugh recalling those calamities because it takes the edge off the darker memories.

One day last year, while I was out on a county tour of a system of Iowa water trails that had been proposed for the Des Moines area, we were riding down the river on a pontoon boat, and I was suddenly overcome with nostalgia for Dad's old Glastron boat. It was so silent out there. I remarked to the man sitting next to me that it was a shame kids today didn't have as many opportunities to be out in nature—and they didn't seek them out, with their obsession with iPads and phones and video games. "Yes," he replied, "it's so calming and peaceful out here. It's good for mental health." And he said something else that really resonated with me—that our kids' mental health could be improved by nature, just taking a deep breath in the shade of a tree, or riding down a river or running through an open field, the grass tickling their toes. As much as we may dismiss the "old ways," a big part of me thinks that's the way life is supposed to be.

As I think back on my life as a farm girl, I realize that the farm was an excellent training ground for the adult challenges I've faced in the military and public office. On the farm, every person is part of a larger purpose. Through all the hardships, we worked together for a harvest that made us proud and contributed to the life of our community and the nation. The lessons of working hard and doing for others helped define me as the person I am today.

Chapter Two

LOST . . .
AND THEN FOUND

Neither of my parents attended college, but they made a point of telling me that I would be going. That was not such a stretch. I loved school. If I was sick, I didn't care—I went anyway. I was one of a tight-knit community of students, twenty-four total in my class. I had almost perfect attendance records, only missing a day in kindergarten for the chicken pox and maybe a half a day as a senior for some reason or another. When it came time to think about college, my teachers engaged me in ways my parents couldn't. They signed me up for programs and advanced classes like college-level genetics. We didn't have a lot of programs in rural Iowa at the time, so that was a big deal.

My education and future were running ahead on one track of my life. But there was a track running in the opposite direction as well—I fell in love.

When I started dating my boyfriend in my junior year of high school, I was ecstatic. I was the last of my friends to date, and my secret fear was that no one would ever love me. I was ashamed of my looks—the braces and Coke-bottle glasses were not exactly a magnet for boys, and neither was my quiet, studious personality. Most of my classmates saw me as sort of a sister, a nice girl who went out of her way to take care of everybody else. So, when one boy from another school district started to take notice, I was beside myself with joy. Rereading my journal from that year, I recognize my starry-eyed self—"I can't stop thinking about him!" We became joined at the hip, and at last I knew what it was like to be in love.

But soon I had a darker secret to keep. The love of my life was abusive. It started in small ways, with controlling behavior. We always had to do what he wanted to do, when he wanted to do it. If I objected or asserted myself in any way, he'd become angry or withdrawn, punishing me for what he saw as my defiance. One time he became so furious with me that he hit me in front of one of my friends. She refused to ever speak to him again, and I should have seen it as a giant warning sign. Instead, I kept making excuses. I obsessively examined my own behavior, looking for ways I could be a better girlfriend who wouldn't make him so mad. I was terrified of losing him. I was inexperienced and naïve. I didn't fully understand that I had a choice not to be treated badly, and I hid my feelings from everyone around me.

We all understand that teenage girls are impressionable. That was me. I gave my boyfriend the upper hand, even though he wasn't outgoing. He wasn't supportive of me. When I was accepted at Iowa State University, I was so happy, but he made it clear he didn't like that I planned to go away to college. He often told me that my opinions were absurd. Thankfully, I was somehow able to summon the nerve to ignore his pleas that I stay home, and made plans for my first year in college.

Iowa State University is in Ames—two and a half hours from Stanton. I had decided to study psychology. My boyfriend would be staying behind, but we were still very much "together," and would see each other on my visits home.

My first semester went well, and I was happily pursuing my dreams. To be honest, it was a relief to be on my own. At a distance, it was easier for me to brush off my boyfriend's disapproval. But then things took a dangerous turn.

Back at home over a weekend in my second semester, I was visiting my boyfriend at his family home one night when he raped me. I was sickened and traumatized, and also felt overwhelmed with guilt. After that, I tried to break up with him. He became very agitated and threatened that if I left him, he'd kill himself. He was not only abusive, but also manipulative.

I was so ashamed when it happened that I could not bring myself to tell my mother or sister or even my best friend. When I returned to college, I called the sexual assault counseling center's hotline, and was encouraged to report the rape to the authorities. I refused. I couldn't stomach the idea that my rape would become public knowledge. I was sure my boyfriend would find a way to blame me. He might even say I wanted it, and I couldn't bear that. It would be decades before I shared the story of my assault publicly. Today I can't stand when people criticize rape victims for not coming forward sooner, because I understand perfectly well why they choose not to.

Instead of confronting the trauma, I buried it and stayed with him. I pasted a smile on my face and pretended nothing was wrong, while the pain festered like an undetected cancer. It was a hard time. I began to struggle with my coursework, and my grades dropped. I had once loved school, but suddenly I couldn't focus. I felt no joy in my daily activities. Internally, I struggled, but I acted as if everything was okay.

Now, looking back, I can clearly see the way this relationship crushed my spirit. I was lost—and then, thanks to a lucky opportunity, I was found again. I was given a lifeline.

One of my mother's best friends belonged to the Farm Bureau, and she read an ad in the *Farm Bureau Spokesman* about a two-week agricultural exchange to Ukraine sponsored by the Iowa Peace Institute. The exchange was open to students, and to apply we had to write an essay about why the exchange was important to us. Although my boyfriend was opposed to me going anywhere, much less outside the United States, I decided to go for it.

I wrote about the importance of keeping an open mind and learning to work together regardless of the differences between our countries. It was a good message for the times. It was 1989, and President Ronald Reagan and Soviet leader Mikhail Gorbachev were engaged in high-profile negotiations to reduce nuclear arms. For the first time since World War II, our two superpowers were reaching out to each other. The exchange was a small part of that opening. Ukraine, which had experienced economic blight and the disaster of the Chernobyl meltdown in 1986, was just beginning to find its voice.

We would be staying on collective farms and working alongside our Ukrainian host families. I was selected, and eighteen of us flew out of Des Moines for Ukraine in the summer of 1989. We were excited, but we didn't know what to expect. Our orientation was fairly minimal, and language would be a barrier. We were all clutching Russian-English dictionaries, and we were accompanied by a translator, a Georgetown University student named Eric Johnson, who knew the language.

We flew to Moscow (my first time flying), where we were met by our Ukrainian escorts and spent a day sightseeing before boarding a train for the fourteen-hour trip to Kyiv. I had never traveled on a train before. It was an old Soviet-style train. We all had little sleeper cars, but I couldn't sleep. I plastered my face against the window, not wanting to miss anything.

At one point, a couple of men approached us. They wanted to buy one of the girls on the trip! She was a cute blonde with a bubbly personality. We stared in shock as Eric cried, "No, no, no, no." They finally went away.

In Kyiv, we boarded buses for a long journey to the May 1st Collective Farm at Lozovatka, named for the symbolic date when collectivization was launched, where our host families were waiting to greet us. Each of us would be staying in a different home.

My family was composed of a mother, her widowed mother, their daughter, Svetlana, a couple of years younger than me, and Igor, a ten-year-old boy. Svetlana was my "little sister" in the exchange. There was no father in the picture—they were divorced or separated. The mother worked as a nurse at the local clinic, and the grandmother—babushka—cared for the children.

Communication was difficult, but we did our best. The family spoke Ukrainian and Russian, which are similar dialects, and the children learned German as a second language in school. I spoke English and high school–level French, which didn't help much. I relied heavily on my Russian-English dictionary, and tried to piece together what I could about my family.

Their little house was a single-story white stucco structure, with only two bedrooms. Svetlana and I shared one, and her mother, grandmother, and Igor slept in the other. Their small kitchen didn't have appliances and there was no indoor plumbing. One of my chores was to go out first thing in the morning and collect buckets of water. We would use those throughout the day for hand washing, dish washing, and the like. We didn't bathe a lot—maybe once or twice while I was there. We'd stand in a basin of water in the kitchen and wash off as best we could.

There was no toilet paper in the outhouse, but to my surprise there was heavy graph paper to do the job, similar to what we used in math class. That amazed and puzzled me. At the end of each day we'd take the bucket and dump it in the field. It was minimalist hygiene, and very different from what I was used to.

My family had a television, but no refrigerator. A root cellar behind the house held items that had to be kept cold—or, I should say, cool. They were never really cold, at least not in the summer while I was there. They bought most of their staples at the market, depending on what was available. After a long wait in line, they'd take whatever was left when they got to the counter. Sometimes they'd have to get milk from a neighbor in trade because they didn't have a cow. The milk would sit on a counter in a covered jar, and it would often be curdled by the time we drank it. I remember straining the curds out with my teeth.

Fortunately, the family was able to supplement their food from the farm. They had a hog pen behind their house and a chicken coop. I worked with the hogs—something I knew how to do. There were also lots of fruits and vegetables. It was tomato season when we were there. During the day, we'd go out and harvest tomatoes by hand, loading them into horse-drawn wagons. There were no tractors. It was very simple—much the way Iowa would have been in the early part of the twentieth century.

Throughout the day there were small snacks, like lemon bars, available on the kitchen counter in case we got hungry. If we were going to be away from the farm, we'd receive lunch wrapped in a cloth—a cured sausage, hunk of cheese, and a roll or bread. Very different from my usual bologna sandwich with mayo and mustard.

One of the trips we took off the farm was to a nearby agricultural fair, similar to our county fair back home. We arrived as a group, and then were able to walk around with our sister or brother. Svetlana and I toured the fair, and she introduced me to many aspects of local agriculture. I learned that Ukraine, with its rich soil, was considered "the breadbasket of Eastern Europe," supplying much of the grain other nations needed.

Collective farming was instituted as a way to increase production and give everyone an equal place in the economy, but even to our untrained eyes this didn't seem to be the result. Everyone worked on the large collective farm, which seemed to be in a constant struggle for survival. The people were very poor. I thought I'd seen poverty in Iowa, but this was another level. Although we had all experienced our share of struggles on Iowa farms, we had the benefits of owner-ship and the promise of self-determination that democracy gave us. Some of our Ukrainian friends whispered to us that they planned to study hard and escape the grim future of working on the collective farms.

One day we took a trip to Kyiv, leaving on a bus very early in the morning, along with our Ukrainian sisters and brothers. Svet-lana had never before left the collective or been on a bus, so it was new to her. She got sick on the bus and the driver had to pull over. Svetlana's family didn't have a car—they just rode bikes or walked everywhere—so I guess the motion of the bus was a shock to her system.

She was fine by the time we got to the city.

Eric was with us to interpret, along with a local couple who spoke English. They described what we were seeing. I vividly remember the way they would point out particular people and tell us, "That man is keeping an eye on us." It was very "old Soviet," and I have to admit it gave us a little thrill.

We saw beautiful churches, but mostly a lot of rubble. It was a sobering reality. Many areas of the city had not yet been rebuilt after World War II—and this was 1989! But the memories of that war, when the United States and the Soviet Union were allies, were still fresh for many of the people. Walking through a field we came upon an elderly cattle herder. Our guides told us he was a survivor of the war who had been a prisoner of the Germans. Eric took us over and introduced us, telling him we were from America. He started to cry, and then he embraced each one of us, kissing our cheeks with tears falling down his face. It wasn't a normal thing for people to be so emotional, but his mind and heart were in a time some forty-plus years earlier, when Americans helped free him.

The spirit of unity with America was present elsewhere, too. In one small park, there was a statue dedicated to a young American girl named Samantha Smith. In 1982, Smith had famously written a letter to Yuri Andropov, who was the Soviet leader before Gorbachev. She had written:

> Dear Mr. Andropov,
>   My name is Samantha Smith. I am 10 years old. Congratulations on your new job. I have been worrying about Russia and the United States getting into a nuclear war. Are you going to vote to have a war or not? If you aren't please tell me how you are going to help to not have a war. This question you do not have to answer, but I would like it if you would. Why do you want to conquer the world or at least our country? God made the world for us to share and take care of. Not to fight over or have one group of people own it all. Please let's do what he wanted and have everybody be happy too.
>
>   Samantha Smith

Smith, who was from Maine, received international attention after Andropov responded to her letter. He assured her, "We want peace—there is something that we are occupied with: growing wheat, building and inventing, writing books and flying into space. We want peace for ourselves and for all peoples of the planet. For our children and for you, Samantha." Then he invited her and her family to visit him in Moscow. They accepted and spent two weeks as Andropov's guests, and it was viewed as a sign of easing relations. In the end, though, no progress would be made until Andropov was gone and Gorbachev was in office. Sadly, Samantha died in a plane crash in 1985, but her memory lived on, even in this tiny Ukrainian park.

In the evenings, there would be gatherings at an auditorium with our host families. The American students would sit up front in a panel, and people asked us questions. Any community member could ask a question, and all of their questions were about what it's like to be an American. That's all they wanted to know. They asked, "What is democracy?" They asked about our government and about our life-styles. We were supposed to be talking about farming, but the con-versations steered away from agriculture into less sanctioned territory.

I remember one such gathering, in particular, where Eric was kept busy during a lively conversation.

"What is it like to be free?" a man asked.

His question opened the floodgates. We couldn't keep up with the questions they threw at us after that. They wanted to know about our government system, what it was like to travel without having to gain permission first, how it felt to be an American. The room was full of subversive energy. We knew that we shouldn't be discussing these topics, that they were off-limits as far as the Soviet Union was concerned, but we did it anyway. The people were eager to hear about how we lived, and their questions revealed a deep unhappiness with the restrictive nature of their lives and how the communist dream had failed them. There was a sense of a fundamental shift happening, although no one knew that only two years later the Soviet Union would collapse, and soon after that, the state-sanctioned collective farming system would come to an end.

We were there as an agricultural exchange, but it was more of a bridge-building exercise between Ukraine and the United States. All of us talked about how we grew up, and our lives, and the opportunities ahead of us. Our Ukrainian families seemed to relish those conversations.

It became even more meaningful the following year when our Ukrainian brothers and sisters visited Iowa. We met them at the airport in Des Moines. It was a very different arrangement because we didn't live in a collective, but were rather all over the state. Three girls, including Svetlana, were assigned to live with my family on our little farm north of Stanton.

That first night in Des Moines we all stayed in a church basement. We ordered pizza, thinking our guests would love it. What kid doesn't love pizza? But they wouldn't eat it. The sausage, spices, and pepperoni were too much for them.

One of the parents went out and bought Campbell's beef soup and made a big pot. They were happy with that.

At our farm, I taught Svetlana how to drive, although she might not have a chance to use that skill. She was actually intimidated by driving a car, but she loved driving our lawn mower. She'd hop on and travel a quarter mile up the road to the neighbor's farm, and from a distance she'd take pictures of our farm—the house, the barn, the bins, the equipment, the fields—so she could show her family back home.

We took the girls to visit Nick's Farm Equipment, which was run by good friends of our parents. Nick sold tractors and other farm implements. We walked around, looking at all the combines and tractors, and our guests climbed up onto the tractors. Their faces said it all. They'd never seen anything like it in their own fields.

One day we took our Ukrainian guests to Kmart. They were overwhelmed. I noticed tears in the eyes of Svetlana and her friends as they looked at the cosmetic display cases, perfumes, and racks and racks of clothing. Back on the collective, and even when we went into Kyiv, there were only a few shops, and you always had to stand in line. There might be only one or two items in the display case, and that was it. We had noticed that most of the boys had the exact same shirt, with little cartoon soccer players on it. They didn't have choices. At Kmart, there were no lines. They could just go to a rack and hold up a dress and take it to the dressing room to try on. Svetlana pulled out a piece of paper with a tracing of Igor's foot on it. We matched it as closely as we could to a boy's pair of tennis shoes. She was so happy with the new shoes for her brother.

The whole experience changed me. I was very aware of my good fortune. I had choices that Svetlana and the others could only dream of—not only what I wore but who I could become. While I was free to do anything that I wanted with my life, they were constrained. Most of them were born on collectives and believed their futures would end there.

I remember thinking, "Hey, I'm going to college, and most of the kids here probably won't." It made me sad, because I could see their hunger for a different way of life. It wasn't just the abundance we had in Iowa, although that certainly impressed them. It was the freedom to imagine your future on your own terms. And more than that, the ability to play a role in shaping your government. I'd always been a proud American, but it made me that much more grateful for the opportunities in our country when I saw what it was like to live in another. I decided that I couldn't take my freedom for granted as I always had. I think the seeds of my future public service were sown in the awakening that came from that exposure to a wider world.

But perhaps what made the greatest difference to me personally was my conversations with our interpreter, Eric. When I left for the exchange, I was in a period of personal crisis. My self-esteem had been battered by my boyfriend. I didn't think much of myself at that time. But this young man, so full of confidence and stories about his studies in Washington, D.C., made a deep impression on me. He was very interested in talking about my studies, and he encouraged me to go for more.

Eric's supportive attitude blew me away—I wasn't used to that. He suggested, "Why don't you get a second degree to psychology—something in business or government? A double major is a great path."

I was taken aback. "Wow, do you think I can?"

Eric said, "Of course! You can do it."

So, here was a nice young man, who was well educated, who was going to a school outside Iowa. He'd seen the world. And he was encouraging me and recognizing my ability. He was saying, "You have the intelligence to do more than x. You can do x, y, and z." I had never been encouraged in this way by a boy who was practically my peer. My boyfriend was the opposite. He tried to control me, because the more educated I became, the further I was moving away from him.

If Eric could believe in me, then so should I. I realized that I had a lot of work to do on myself. It was as if a light went on in my mind. I remember thinking, "I can't live like this anymore. I can't tolerate this." And so, after returning from Ukraine, I finally had the courage to break up with my boyfriend once and for all.

For me, developing self-esteem was a process. It didn't happen overnight. I'd always taken everything so deeply to heart. I'd judged myself harshly, assuming I wasn't capable of lofty aspirations. I'd convinced myself that being ordinary was okay, and being in a relationship meant taking second place. Now, armed with a new spark of inspiration, I decided to seek more from my life.

SERVICE

Service has been a foundation for me since I was young. I've served in the military. I've served fellow survivors of abuse. I've been a political servant, trying my best to represent Iowa and its people. Service to me means helping people where you can. It means self-sacrifice and hard decisions. It's not easy to put your personal concerns on hold and give yourself to others. I've learned the art of service over the years from the incredible people around me who all believe that there's something worth fighting for.

Here's a secret about service: In the process of doing for others I became enriched myself. Through service I found my power. People might look at me today—a military veteran, a U.S. senator—and think I was born brave and bold. But I didn't come to it naturally. I understand from my own experience that even strong women like me can have a hard time learning to appreciate their worth. When I was a young woman I might have been brave enough to castrate hogs, but there were times in life when it was hard for me to simply stand up for myself. Serving in the military showed me I was capable of personal fortitude, and that allowed me to be a strong advocate for others.

Chapter Three

FOR LOVE OF COUNTRY

Once I was back at Iowa State University in my second year, freed from my abusive boyfriend and enlivened by my Ukrainian experience, my thoughts turned to service. Military service hadn't really been a large part of my family's life when I was growing up. Dad didn't talk much about his brief military service, and only one person, my mother's younger brother, was an Army lifer. But I had a couple of dorm mates who were in the Reserve Officer Training Corps (ROTC) at our school, and my friend Dave Trotter urged me, "Just sign up for a couple of classes and see what you think." I decided to try it. I took a couple of military science classes, and I loved them. I fit right in. So I signed a contract and was given a two-year scholarship that covered all of my expenses at Iowa State.

My family was nervous about me joining ROTC. My father had been a sergeant in the Iowa Army National Guard back in his day (a mechanic in the same company that I would go on to command in Operation Iraqi Freedom), and he warned me not to get on my sergeant's bad side—to keep my head down and my nose clean. He thought the military would be hard on me, and prevent me from growing into myself. The opposite was true. I found that I welcomed the challenge. ROTC is a very demanding program. I learned military skills, leadership training, discipline, and career training all in one package. I loved it and loved the people I served with. I realized that I had been looking for a way to be fully engaged in a larger purpose, and my service would change my life.

For the first time in college, I found myself really working hard to achieve something, to prove that I was worthy. I immersed myself in a community of similar people who all wanted to support our country. The other ROTC students became a sort of second family to me while I was there. I had to face my own fears and challenge myself beyond what I thought were my limits.

So that's what I did. I drilled down and believed that I could tackle this tremendous task I'd put in front of myself. Something surprising happened. I was happy! I worked alongside my fellow ROTC members and couldn't have had a better time. The challenges shaped me into a leader, and the friendships have lasted a lifetime.

I reported to Fort Knox, Kentucky, for my initial ROTC basic training course, which cadets go through. It wasn't full-blown basic training like enlisted soldiers undergo, but it was physically hard and mentally challenging. I'd played sports growing up, so I could hold my own on the physical side of things, but I'd finish every day completely exhausted.

Very early in the morning, while it was still dark, we'd gather outside for PT exercises—push-ups, flutter kicks, and cardio training, finishing with a long run of several miles, all with a drill sergeant shouting orders. PT also had a way of following us throughout the day. If you got a task wrong, down you'd go for twenty push-ups.

Most of our time was divided into training blocks, such as rifle marksmanship. I had handled guns before, so I had a little bit of an advantage over some of the others, but I still had to learn to quickly break down, clean, and load my rifle and excel at target practice, including shooting a target while lying in a prone position. We learned everything step by step, followed by practical exercises that mimicked what we might experience in the field.

For me, the toughest practical exercise was the chemical training. It felt deadly real as we learned to put on our MOPP (Mission-Oriented Protective Posture) suits, knowing that in case of a chemical attack, a poorly fitted suit could be deadly. The final step in that training was enduring exposure. They sent us into a gas chamber where they would release CS gas, which is nonlethal but still pretty awful. In the chamber, we were instructed to remove our masks and start singing "America the Beautiful." We got the first few words out, but as soon as the gas hit us we started choking and wheezing and drooling. Fairly quickly they'd send us out and tell us to flap our arms to get the gas off our suits. We were a mess, with snot pouring out of our noses and saliva dripping from our mouths. Our eyes burned. I would perform this exercise many times in my military career, and it never got any easier.

From sunup until sundown we focused on these basic soldiering skills, and when we weren't doing that we were mopping and waxing and performing general chores. In the women's barracks, there was a crumbling layer of wax on the floor, and our drill sergeant ordered us to get down on our hands and knees and scrape the wax off with tiny razor blades. Obviously, we could have buffed it off with a machine, but the exercise was designed to teach us humility and patience—how to tolerate the mundane indignities that are part of military life out in the field.

It was a thousand times more rigorous than the ROTC training I was used to back at Iowa State. The drill sergeants would get right in your face and scream at you. I knew they did it to prepare us for hardships down the road, and to instill discipline, but it was hard to stomach. One instance sticks out to me more than any other.

Each platoon was assigned its own office area in one hallway below the barracks. As I was on CQ (charge of quarters) one night, I could hear a commotion outside of my platoon area. Out in the hallway was an enraged drill sergeant screaming at a young male cadet—he was probably 6'3" and 210 pounds. The young man was crying. Tears were streaming down his cheeks as the drill sergeant continued his tirade of profanities. The young man was begging to go home; he didn't want to be in the Army. I felt so badly for him. I stared as the drill sergeant ripped him apart with mere words. I saw this strong young man being publicly humiliated by a virtual stranger. When the sergeant was done, I stepped back into my platoon's office and took a deep breath.

While I loved my time at Fort Knox and in ROTC, I swore to myself that I would never be like either one of those individuals—the drill sergeant, harsh and unyielding; or the cadet, weeping and shamed in the face of adversity.

During my college years, I was involved in extracurricular work, volunteering at a safe house for battered and abused women and children. It was an experience that would make a lifelong impression on me. It opened my eyes to the reality that domestic abuse could happen to anyone, even privileged women who lived in beautiful houses. I knew that a lot of people thought abused women were stupid to stay with their husbands or partners, and by doing so they deserved what they got. But because of my rape experience, I had a special compassion for them beyond my years. I knew that it wasn't their fault; it was the abuser's fault. I also understood why so many of them decided to stay—the incidents that brought them to the safe house were never the first abuse. Typically, the abuse had been going on for a long time, until they were in such fear that they made the choice to flee their abusers, to save themselves and their children, even though that meant leaving everything behind. I was in awe of their courage, and I suffered for their pain. I carried a beeper at all times, and very often the call would come in the late hours of the night, pulling me out of bed to the hospital, jail, or shelter where another family was in crisis. I could not have imagined then that I would one day share their plight—but that was a long time away.

I met my future husband, Gail, late in my college career. He was seventeen years older than I, divorced with two daughters, and he was a supervisor with the Ranger Challenge Team, which was a competitive team that focused on strength, speed, and military skills.

I didn't know him that well, but I thought he was a nice guy and good-looking—a career Army man. We'd talk in passing. By then I was dating a classmate, but it wasn't very serious. We were getting ready to graduate, and decided it was time to go our separate ways. Shortly after my graduation, to my surprise, Gail asked me out on a date. I was dumbfounded that this mature, accomplished man would see something in me. Even though I was a much stronger, self-confident woman than I had been three years earlier, to be honest, I was in awe of him. He radiated a sense of purpose and was an example of the military person I aspired to be. But although I was young, it wasn't a one-way admiration. Gail often spoke of what he saw in me—my energy, my commitment, and even my courage. I was elated to be in such a mutually respectful relationship.

Within a few months, we were inseparable. The question of our future was settled quickly. The summer following my graduation, Gail was being assigned to the First Ranger Battalion in Savannah, Georgia, and he asked me to come with him. I told him straight out, "I'm not going to live with a man unless I have a ring on my finger." As the date approached for Gail to leave, he proposed. I was absolutely in love with him, and I accepted. It was so unlike me. I had always been overly cautious, but here I was certain.

So we got engaged and moved to Savannah. Before long, we'd be torn apart again, because I now had my military career, too. I had joined the Army Reserves, and I was scheduled to leave in a few months for my Officer Basic Course in Fort Leonard Wood, Missouri. I tried to get a counseling position in the meantime, but the short time frame discouraged employers, so I took a part-time job at the mall to help pay the bills. During that time, Gail and I secretly got married because the Rangers were on hard cycles of training and exercises, and could be deployed at a moment's notice. The chaplain at Gail's unit performed the ceremony in the battalion command sergeant major's office, and we didn't tell anyone. We had an "official" wedding scheduled back home in Iowa the next summer. After I completed my Engineer Officer Basic Course at Fort Leonard Wood, we joined family and friends at my home church in Stanton for a joyous wedding. It was during the summer floods of 1993, and it had been raining all week. The sun broke through for the wedding, and the rain returned later that night.

It was a military wedding. The servicemen wore their dress-blue uniforms and the women wore off-the-shoulder navy blue dresses. We had a saber cordon as we exited the church. It was beautiful—my dream wedding. We had a cake reception in the church basement, then the crowd moved to my parents' farm for a hog roast in the machine shed. While they never questioned my judgment, I'm sure my folks worried about me marrying a man who was so much older than me.

Gail had received new orders, and we'd be moving to Fort Benning, Georgia. I decided to start a master's program in public administration at Columbus College. While taking classes, I got a part-time job selling women's and children's shoes at the mall.

I was also serving in the Reserves. The Reserves involves being in a part-time unit, with a requirement to drill one weekend a month, plus a two-week block for annual training. However, we were required to be ready for deployment if the federal government called us to active duty. Reserves soldiers receive the same training as active-duty soldiers, so we're always prepared. Although being in the Reserves allows us to pursue civilian careers, it is always our first obligation.

Once I received my master's, I got a job on the Army post, counseling soldiers who were exiting the military. I helped them with job coaching, networking, writing resumes, and even how to dress—all of those things that young soldiers really don't know anything about. It was a wonderful job, because I felt I was helping provide a valuable service. Most of these soldiers had joined when they were quite young, and their time in the military had been regimented. They were used to being told what to do every step of the way—salute and follow orders. Now they were facing the world on their own, and many of them were insecure.

The most common question I got was "What if I don't find a job?" That was followed by a series of other "what ifs" that swirled around in their heads. I came to see helping them as a mission more than a job, because what could be more worthwhile than helping veterans find happiness and success after they had served their country?

It was my role to make sure they were as prepared as possible for life out there beyond the military. To boost their confidence as much as I could. To walk them through the interviews they'd be facing in their search for employment. I'd videotape them in mock interviews and I'd be brutal in my evaluations: *Don't answer like that, look me in the eye, smile, be confident.* I'd tell them, "You're not in the Army now. Here's what civilian employers expect." It was grueling, but we kept rehearsing until they got it. By the time most of them walked out, I could see the new confidence in their postures.

I also addressed the crucial question of how they could translate their military skills into general life. Our military is a highly skilled force. These men and women had a range of abilities that they often didn't appreciate. I kept a book with all of the military occupational skills in it. So, if a soldier said, "I was 92 Golf," which is the code for a military cook, I would walk them through the skill set—the equipment they knew how to use and the food they cooked—and show them how to incorporate their abilities into a résumé. Leadership skills were also highlighted.

It wasn't just the skills that were beneficial. I urged them to think about the special qualities they could bring to the job as a result of their service, such as experience with teamwork, a strong work ethic, and high motivation.

One would think that any employer would be delighted to have employees with these qualities, but sometimes former soldiers had trouble convincing people that their skills were really transferable, and that they could cope with a less rigid civilian occupation. I tried to break through these stereotypes. It bears mentioning that military veterans still face discrimination in the job market today. Some employers are happy to say, "Thank you for your service," and then conclude veterans are not a good fit, especially if they've suffered from post-traumatic stress. We have an obligation to make this right for our veterans.

I felt as if I had the best of everything. I was married to a man in the military, I was serving in the Army Reserves and had my own unit, and I was supporting soldiers. When I was younger, I never imagined I would live away from home, but now I was traveling. Not every post had a Job Assistance Center, so twice I went to Fort Buchanan in San Juan, Puerto Rico, to counsel soldiers, and I also went to MacDill Air Force Base in Tampa, Florida. Life with Gail also involved regular moves. Our next posting was at Fort Jackson in Columbia, South Carolina. I actually enjoyed the moves, loved meeting new people, and quickly adapted to the military lifestyle.

In Columbia, I got a job with Blue Cross/Blue Shield as a tester-trainer, working with job applicants to test and improve their job skills. For example, I'd give writing skills tests and grade them on content, grammar, and punctuation. I'd never thought much about it, but writing skills are pretty important for most jobs. From there, I secured a position at Midlands Technical College, which was similar to my previous job at Fort Benning. This was my wheelhouse, working with long-term unemployed people who needed new skills. I could relate to their struggles because I had seen them in the farm communities. Some folks I knew back home had never done anything else but farm. But when they'd lose their farms and have to get other jobs, they'd often be at a loss about how to translate those very specific skills. People didn't want to think their only choices were low-paying retail jobs in town. A lot of the unemployed folks we dealt with in South Carolina had operated denim looms, which had seemed like a pretty secure occupation. But their companies were computerizing and replacing humans with technology, and they were laying off workers. There was great hardship in the community, and our program was their lifeline.

At the technical school, we were dealing with low-skilled workers who were trying to elevate their prospects with computer degrees or with certified nursing certificates. My job was to help them find employment once they developed a set of skills. It was extremely satisfying when we succeeded. Our program even received a national award for our success. It made a deep impression on me, which I carried all the way to the Senate. It's one thing to talk about unemployment as a statistical abstraction. It's another to get down in the trenches and truly understand what people are facing, and find ways to help them.

When Gail and I decided to get married, we'd had a conversation about children, which was our first disagreement. I wanted children.

Gail, who already had two nearly grown daughters, didn't want more children. Ultimately, we decided to put off the decision—which is not something I'd recommend, by the way. Privately, I agonized over it. I didn't want Gail to feel as if I was forcing him into it. But I wanted children.

We let it go for a few years, and finally when I was twenty-eight, I broached the subject: "I would really love to have a child soon." I was thrilled when Gail agreed. The compromise was that there would be only one. He was taking a new assignment in Saudi Arabia at the time, so it looked as if it would have to wait, but to my delight I got pregnant during his mid-tour leave.

For the first six months of my pregnancy, I was alone in South Carolina, working full-time at the college. I also had my reserve unit in Fort Jackson, and I was keeping up our three-bedroom ranch house. I was busy, but lonely. To fill what free time I did have, I began volunteering at a VA nursing home on Sundays and a couple of evenings a week. I fed the veterans, took them to chapel, and sat and talked with them.

There were men of all eras at the nursing home—World War II, Korea, and present-day veterans. One young man whose foster mother became a close friend had suffered greatly when he had been involved in a vehicle accident that left him with a serious brain injury. His foster mom told me about his rough childhood and how he had become a military policeman to help others. Now it took great effort to move him from his bed into his wheelchair. The simplest things were complicated, and he couldn't do them on his own. There was an older African American veteran who could not speak, and his hands—twisted and gnarly—struggled to hold a spoon. I would help feed him his supper, and I saw in his eyes that he appreciated my efforts.

One of the World War II veterans was a small man with a boy's face. I could tell that at one time he had been very handsome. He did not speak much, typical for the men on that floor, but he loved to walk! I would hold him steady as we walked laps around and around the floor. He would cry often, but I understood it was the side effect from a long-ago stroke.

Another thirtysomething man had also suffered a stroke, and was confined to a wheelchair. He used a board with letters on it to spell out the words he wanted to say. He enjoyed a kiss on the cheek as I said my good-byes. These men were lonely. I understood.

With my first baby on the way, I was going to doctor's appointments by myself, which was hard. I was alone for my first sonogram, when I learned we were having a girl. I was elated, but a little worried, too. I knew Gail had hoped for a boy, and I wondered if he'd be very disappointed when he called from Saudi Arabia and got the news. I was worried for nothing. He assured me he was quite happy and excited about welcoming our little girl.

Six months into my pregnancy, Gail came home, but we'd be leaving right away for his new assignment at the Ranger Camp at Eglin Air Force Base. I had already sold the house and scheduled the movers. If that seems like fast work, well, welcome to military life. Moving is almost second nature—at least, it had become that way for us. In Florida, I had to find a new doctor, whom I'd meet only once before I delivered. I was halfway through the Lamaze classes when I went into labor, a week before my due date. It was fast for a first baby, or so they told me. My water broke, and two and a half hours later, Libby was born.

Libby was the light and joy of our lives. She was also colicky. She slept pretty well at night, but she cried all day long. Gail was working long hours, so I was often alone in the house, struggling with breastfeeding a baby who could not be comforted, and feeling very discouraged. I worried that I was doing it all wrong.

Fortunately, I got through it, and also early teething—Libby had four teeth come in all at once. But after that, she transformed into the happiest baby in the world. It was a big relief! She had an effervescent laugh, and it was like music to hear. She was so beautiful, and very chubby. We called her Chubbo Bubbo, and Gail joked that she looked like the Michelin Man.

I'd never felt as much appreciation for military life as I did when I had a baby. Suddenly I had a built-in parenting community of officers' wives and enlisted women. Our children were all around the same age. The Ranger Camp where we lived was located on a training range in the middle of the woods on Eglin Air Force Base. It was a long way from civilization, about twenty-five miles from town. If the Air Force was doing flyovers with live ammunition they had to close the roads, which happened regularly. Security police posted notices on our doors and we had to plan our trips to town according to military bombing runs. So we were isolated. However, we had a wonderful, supportive community, and Libby had plenty of little friends to play with. Our homes were situated around a circular area with a gazebo, and on most days, we'd all come out with our kids and socialize together while they ran around the yard. I no longer felt so alone in figuring out motherhood. There were plenty of friends ready to help me out.

During that period I was a stay-at-home mom. I was still in the Reserves, but I didn't drill regularly with a unit. I was what was called an RMA—a Reserve Mobilization Augmentee. I did my annual training wherever there was a slot open. In that year, I spent my two weeks in Kansas City, filling in at the federal building with the Army Corps of Engineers.

When Libby was a year and a half, Gail and I moved back to Red Oak, Iowa—my first time living at home in nine years. Gail was retiring from the military and getting a civilian job. We bought a house in Red Oak that had belonged to one of my best childhood friends, and the sense of familiarity and belonging was strong.

When we moved home, I decided to transfer from the Reserves to the Iowa National Guard. As long as Gail was in the military, the Reserves had made more sense because it was a federal program. But once we settled in Iowa, where we planned to stay, the National Guard, controlled by the governor, was more appealing.

I had a deeper motivation for joining the Guard—a desire to give back and be part of something that differentiated me from everyone else. I made a conscious decision that I was willing to lay it all on the line for people who would probably never know me, whether that meant supporting communities through natural disasters or security emergencies or even going to war. Older and wiser, my calculations were different than when I joined the Reserves. My choice wasn't about getting college benefits or even about being heroic. I understood the risks and I didn't take them lightly.

I started out as a supply officer for a battalion, and did that for about a year before moving to the 1168th Transportation Company, which supported the logistical and transportation needs of other companies. The 1168th was split geographically across the western part of Iowa. We had an armory in Red Oak, which housed the headquarters. The armories in Perry and Audubon each supported a truck platoon and a maintenance section.

I was home in Red Oak with two-year-old Libby on September 11, 2001. It was a little chaotic as I had men in the house installing a furnace. A frantic call came from a neighbor: "Turn on your TV."

The furnace installers stopped working and we all stared at the TV as we watched the horror unfold. Along with other Americans, we knew our lives would never be the same. But for those of us in the military, that awareness was all the more intense.

In early 2002, I was informed that I was being promoted to company commander. It was phenomenal to be selected as a young leader in the Guard. That had been my goal, but I hadn't expected it to happen so soon. There was a wonderful change-of-command ceremony in the fall of 2002, with the former commander handing me the company guidon—the flag with our transportation insignia. I was proud that day. There were so few women in leadership positions, and now I was one of them.

The National Guard was a part-time assignment, but being in leadership meant more time and responsibility—doing training schedules, working with the officers at each of the armories, leadership meetings, leadership calls. In this period after 9/11, I was responsible for making sure the 1168th would be ready if called to serve.

Less than 15 percent of our company was female. That was actually high compared to other companies, but it was still very few women. I learned quickly that because it was such a boys' club, I would have to be assertive. I was still nice, but all business. I didn't have female role models, so I had to create my own leadership style.

I was the only woman officer, and at the time I didn't even have senior officers who were women. In fact, I was the first female company commander of that unit. The soldiers mostly seemed fine with it, but some of the older retired guys expressed worries. They'd ask, "Are we going to be okay?" I was determined to show them that we were.

I had to figure out things on my own. One of the colonels who mentored me admitted to me years later that he could have taken a more active role in my training. "I'm sorry about that," he said. "I just didn't know how to mentor a woman."

I told him that it wasn't that I needed a woman mentor. I just needed to know how to be a leader. I think a lot of men get too wrapped up in gender in the military. The way I saw it, a soldier is a soldier. It doesn't matter your gender. You still have the same job to do.

Later, when I was in Washington, I had a visit from a noncommissioned officer (NCO), the first female who went into the infantry for the National Guard. We talked about this question of mentoring. "I don't need somebody to tell me how to be a woman," she said. "I already know how to do that. I need somebody to teach me how to be an infantryman."

In fact, being a woman could be an advantage. Taking care of my troops was an instinct. They were very much like part of my family, and some of the younger kids were almost like my children. I wanted the best for them. I wanted them to behave. I wanted them to work hard. I encouraged them when they needed encouragement. I disciplined them when they needed discipline. And I expressed pride when they did well. The 1168th was ready for anything. We were strong together.

Throughout 2002, we were on edge, knowing that deployment orders could come at any time. The War on Terror in Afghanistan was already in full swing. In November 2002, we started to hear rumors at the 1168th that an assignment was coming. Actually, it was more than a rumor. We were told that all of our wheeled equipment would be going to the paint booths at Camp Dodge and Sioux City to be painted "desert tan." The operation was on a fast track—twenty-four hours a day, seven days a week. Asked about it by reporters, the National Guard deflected with the explanation that the equipment needed painting anyway. That might have satisfied the public, but we in the National Guard knew that this was the first stage toward deployment.

Soon after, I received a call from our Readiness NCO, letting me know about a conversation he'd had with the 68th Corps Support Battalion in Fort Carson, Colorado, asking for information on my company. When the 68th deployed, our company would fall under its purview. It was a pretty big clue. Still, we carried on through the Christmas season with no orders. I focused on my family, cooking, wrapping presents, and decorating the Christmas tree with my bright little three-year-old. By Christmas Eve, as Libby babbled on about Santa Claus, I was pretty sure I would be leaving soon. I concentrated on savoring those precious days with my family.

On January 7, 2003, Secretary of Defense Donald Rumsfeld announced that the United States would be increasing troop numbers in the Middle East. The alert notification for the 1168th came on January 28, and on February 5, our 183 soldiers went up to Camp Dodge from our armories at Red Oak, Perry, and Audubon to begin the administrative process, which also included physicals, immunizations, and legal procedures. That evening I brought everyone together and gave them an official mobilization notification, then released them to call their families. We settled in at our home bases to wait for a call forward to our mobilization station at Fort McCoy, Wisconsin.

The delay was partially due to the sheer mass of military mobilization all over the country. In addition, movement was stalled by Turkey's refusal to allow our military to use its land and air space as a staging ground for sending troops into Iraq. Funneling hundreds of thousands of forces through Kuwait had created a logjam. We were essentially waiting in line.

The call forward finally came on February 24. There were farewell ceremonies in Red Oak, Perry, and Audubon. Our emotional and inspiring Red Oak ceremony was attended by a large crowd of friends, families, neighbors, and fellow service members. Our support organization, the Red Oak Ambassadors, served a beautiful meal, and then I released my soldiers to spend a last night with their families. The next day we'd be up early to begin a two-day convoy to Fort McCoy, where we would have eight weeks of training before shipping out.

Fort McCoy is a vast training camp of sixty thousand acres in eastern Wisconsin, near the Iowa border. The training was very rigorous. We'd set up potential mission scenarios, outsize challenges, and physical dangers. Since we'd be going into combat zones, we had to be just as prepared as the fighting forces. We were also entering a world with a different culture that few of us understood. So, a big part of the training was learning as much as we could about the local customs. It was exhilarating to be pushed so hard, and my troops really rose to the occasion. I was proud of how hard they worked and how much they were sacrificing for this mission. We had single mothers, wives, men with families, and we even had one married couple deploying together. All of them were willing and ready to go and do their duty. They were pitching in to help other Iowans mobilizing throughout Wisconsin. They were real team players and very hard workers. I would attribute that to their Iowa work ethic.

Of course, at the mobilization station, which was very large and full of many units, we encountered different leadership styles and different ways of doing things. For example, some of the other Iowans had decided there would be no drinking at all, even though there was an enlisted club that served beer to soldiers who were of age. But my first sergeant and I talked it through. We decided that as long as the senior NCOs responsible for those soldiers made sure that they were just having a couple of beers, and not overdoing it, we were fine with that. So, in the evenings, once all the rooms were ready and all the training stats were done, they were free to go. We called it turning on the beer light. They could go to the club or have a couple of beers in the barracks.

I bring this up to make the point that when you trust your soldiers—who, after all, are heading to a war zone—you get good behavior in return. Our soldiers didn't get into trouble. They worked hard, took a break, and were back up the next day ready to go. Incidentally, this wasn't always the case with "dry" units. One in particular had a lot of problems with soldiers sneaking out and overdrinking. That seems to me to demonstrate a basic tenet of leadership. Trust your people. Respect them as responsible adults. You'll get positive results.

These men and women were headed to war. Many people think of the Guard as a domestic service, and might be surprised to know that the Iowa National Guard sent nearly ten thousand troops to Iraq through 2007. Some, like the 1168th, served in support roles, including logistics, police, operations, and medical services. There were many air and ground fighting battalions, too. Other states sent their National Guard as well.

After two months training, we were up early on April 18 for transport to Wisconsin's Volk Airfield, where our aircraft was awaiting us. Wheels up at 10:05, and we were on our way to Kuwait.

Chapter Four

WAR ZONE

When we arrived in theater, it was pure chaos. We landed at Kuwait City International Airport on April 19, 2003, and deplaned into a stifling heat. It was spring, but the temperature was in the nineties; when we'd left Fort McCoy, there had been a foot of snow on the ground. Dressed in full combat gear and sweating heavily, we were transported to nearby Camp Wolf, which served as a reception and in-processing center for arriving troops. At Camp Wolf, the waves of heat drenched us, and the soft, powderlike, windswept sand invaded every crevice of our bodies. The result was a constant muddy, itchy discomfort.

There were thousands and thousands of American troops packed in. They were supposed to be sent to their stations within four hours, but because there were so many, there was a backup, leaving units temporarily housed at Camp Wolf, which lacked even rudimentary facilities. The 1168th was stuck there because it was unclear where we would be attached. Originally, we were to be attached to a company that was going to Iraq through Turkey, but after the Turkish government denied America access to its military bases, that route was cut off.

We were hunkered down at Camp Wolf. There were no shower

or hygiene facilities, and we tried to keep clean as best we could. In the humidity, all of us reeked. You'd try to find a private spot to clean up with baby wipes, but it didn't really help. There were porta-potties, but you can imagine after a week it was pretty ripe.

We slept in large cotton Bedouin tents set up by foreign contractors. Our 150 soldiers were housed with other units, 250 to a tent. We were crammed in like sardines in our sleeping bags, with rucksacks as pillows, men and women together. There were no cots. God help you if you had to go to the latrine at night. You'd end up stepping on a number of angry people as you tried to exit the tent.

There wasn't room for our gear in the tents, so we had to leave our supplies and duffels at a staging area under guard. Many in the unit would congregate at the staging area and play cards, read, and hang out together to escape the boredom and claustrophobia of the tents. And it got to a point where it stank so badly in the tents that some soldiers were going out to the staging area and sleeping on top of their duffel bags.

We were basically a company without a home, prevented from doing our job. We just had to wait for the call forward. As the commander, it was up to me to maintain discipline and morale, even though I had little idea of how or when our situation would improve. Looking back, I realize that it was one of my greatest tests of leadership—how to help my men and women stay focused when we were surrounded by chaos. I relied on my training, and vowed to maintain my cool and insist on troop discipline, even in uncertain conditions.

During the long days, I went to the Camp Wolf administrative tent every few hours to find out where we would be assigned. Finally, I established contact with the 541st Maintenance Battalion at Camp Arifjan, about thirty miles away, and began making arrangements to join them there. But Camp Arifjan was overcrowded, too, so we had to wait until there was room. Finally, we were given the go-ahead to make the drive to the camp. We loaded our gear into a cargo truck and boarded buses for the trip.

That thirty-mile drive took several hours, because the drivers weren't familiar with the route and we ended up going in circles looking for the camp. We arrived well after dark.

Camp Arifjan was the largest army post in Kuwait, just south of Kuwait City. It contained four subcamps, named after baseball fields. We were assigned to South Camden Yards, which was a mile from the main gate. Camden Yards was a multinational camp, with more than 500 Ukrainian soldiers in the north and 1,300 American soldiers in the south. There was a camp "mayor" whose command post tent was centrally located.

We were still in tents at the new camp, but we had cots and there were showers—although you couldn't really take a cold shower because the water was hot. Everything was hot there. In some cases, *explosively* hot. One day the little storage building where we kept soft drinks blew up; the heat was that intense. And we were plagued by scorpions. Each morning before we put our boots on, we had to shake them out to avoid a nasty surprise.

On top of that, none of our equipment had arrived. Back home we'd loaded three ships with trucks and trailers, but the harbor was so crowded, there was no room to bring them in and download them at the port. We had to wait until our port call and have soldiers there ready to get the equipment as it came off the ships. We sent soldiers down to the seaport to wait for the ships and they checked every day, but our ships didn't arrive. Our team was camped out in a little concrete culvert, like a bomb shelter, living rough. It would take several weeks for our equipment to finally get there.

Finally, we were ready to roll. Most of our missions were in Kuwait. Our equipment was made for off-road, short-haul missions.

But we ended up doing some long missions up into Iraq, taking supplies to a couple of different logistics spaces and to Baghdad International Airport. A lot of different transportation units were in theater at that time. And we were constantly moving. It got to a point that we really had to be careful because, by regulation, soldiers have to have at least four hours off per day. And that's to sleep.

We were pushing the envelope on four hours of sleep. It was the beginning of the war, so everybody was moving forward into Iraq. It was a nonstop effort getting all those units pushed forward and supplying them.

We were hauling it all. We used to say we hauled everything while we were in theater: Patriot missiles, concrete barriers, sun shades, scud bunkers, containers, refrigerated vans of fresh fruit and vegetables, body armor and tactical vests, medical supplies, bunk beds, mattresses, grills, forklifts, coolers, MREs, guard towers, petroleum, ammunition, tents, clothing, mail, and embalming powder. Always in stifling heat. None of our vehicles were air conditioned, and our truck designs were what they called a cab-over model. This was a flat-front truck with the engine under the seats. We were literally sitting on top of the engine. We'd keep the windows open, but driving fifty miles an hour in 120-degree heat with the sand blowing straight in made for the roughest rides of any of our lives.

A lot of the troops, the guys especially, got rashes because they were sweating so much. It was chafing, uncomfortable. We were also going through boots like crazy—the sweat would run down our legs and pool where our pants were tucked into our boots. This caused salt deposits. Salt and sweat would deteriorate the material of the boots, and so we were swapping out boots frequently. Those ordinary things you never think of until you're there.

Our first convoy into Iraq was on May 5 as part of the 542nd

Maintenance Company's permanent move to Logbase Seitz, just outside of Baghdad. We had three military vehicles with trailers, one Humvee, and one 5-T wrecker. The trucks carried supplies and mail. We started off okay, but we had a heck of a time getting through Kuwait City traffic, and the convoy was split up. We regrouped outside the city, and picked up many other units along the main supply route to Baghdad. At night, we parked at Tallil Air Base and slept in and on top of our vehicles. (Later, soldiers brought hammocks that they'd string between trucks at night, or they put cots in the back of a trailer. I'd sleep on the hood of my Humvee.)

Sometimes while we were driving, little kids would appear from out of nowhere and beg for food. They'd point to their mouths and rub their tummies. Our soldiers were moved by this—I think we all remembered seeing films of American soldiers in World War II tossing candy bars to the children, and feeling warmed by that. When soldiers would toss food to one or two children, more kids would appear from everywhere, dancing around the convoy and begging. We'd heard that a little girl had been run over trying to get a candy bar. So, we made it a hard-and-fast rule: do not throw water or food to these kids because it's too dangerous for them.

It went against my every instinct, but discipline required it. It wasn't our job to relate to the Iraqis. Our job was simply to haul. That went for adults, too. We didn't have interpreters with us and we had no way of knowing whether someone was friend or foe.

Those early months we were constantly moving. Everybody pitched in and they all were so excited to be working and part of the team. A real sign of teamwork was the way our cooks did their part. We had several cooks who came with us, but unbeknownst to us all of the camps in Kuwait had dining facilities already, staffed by third-country nationals. They had standing contracts with providers like Kellogg Brown & Root and other big defense contractors. Our cooks were consigned to the sidelines, doing head counts and overseeing the nationals. They weren't so busy.

Seeing how stretched the transportation crews were, our cooks started volunteering to help out. They'd gather laundry from the truck drivers and wait in line at the laundry trailers and do everyone's laundry—something our drivers didn't have time to do. They'd run errands and go to the PX to fill requests for our drivers. The cooks wanted to be part of the team, even if they weren't cooking. Everyone was highly motivated to work together, and I was proud of them.

While our conditions were rudimentary, they were still better than those of soldiers fighting in Iraq. When we'd packed up our unit back home, we'd thought of everything. We went lock, stock, and barrel. Our unit could have survived on its own. We had toilet seats, sheets of plywood, materials to make our own latrines. We even had hand-crank washing machines, which had been donated by Iowans. Farmers had pulled them out of their barns and sent them with us. Since we had laundry trailers at camp, we sent those hand-crank washers to Iraq with soldiers heading for combat. We enjoyed telling people back home that those Iowa hand-crank washers were supporting units all over Iraq!

The craziest thing was that we didn't have maps to find our way. It was madness. No one thought to supply maps. We made do as best we could, using a hand-drawn map from a Tennessee National Guard transportation company. There were a lot of other trucks on the road. So, we figured, if we ever took a wrong turn somewhere along the line we'd find another unit that was moving north, too. Soldiers were complaining, "How do I find my way to Baghdad Airport?" It seems pretty obvious, pretty basic. Give drivers maps. Eventually, we started drawing our own, figuring out landmarks.

The terrain was desolate. There was a main supply route (MSR) from Kuwait into Iraq, and there was an alternate supply route (ASR). Most of the time we'd take the MSR, but if there were troubles on that route, we'd take the ASR, and it was bumpy and unpaved, with sand everywhere. Basically, we'd be driving through the middle of the desert. All we could see for miles around were sand dunes and junkyard remnants from previous wars.

We were always concerned about explosives and ambushes, but our vehicles weren't armored. Often, the soldiers would take their SAPI plates, the armor plating that goes inside protective vests, and slip them down the sides of the doors. Or they'd sit on them because the blasts would often come from under the vehicle. We'd also line the floors of the vehicles with sand bags, hoping they'd at least partially absorb a blast. We improvised.

The Humvees, which I usually rode in, were harder to retrofit because they had vinyl sides and tops. But sometimes the guys would take off the Humvee doors to give them greater movement if they needed to jump quickly. It's not as if those doors were providing much protection anyway.

At that time, we did not worry as much about the threat of IEDs. Later in my deployment, they were a primary killer. As the war progressed, the Army started up-armoring vehicles and manufacturing heavier vehicles that could withstand blasts. But none of us who were deployed at first had that level of protection. The whole Army was learning in the field, because this was a very different kind of battlefront. Later, when I was in the Senate, I would fight for proactively outfitting men and women serving in those dangerous, unpredictable terrains. I also introduced a bill in 2019 addressing a special issue for women in combat—body armor designed for men that didn't fit them. Poorly fitting body armor was one of the leading causes of injury for women in war zones.

Whenever we halted on the road, we stayed on the road, because we'd been taught that there were booby traps and mines everywhere. There was no wandering around! We'd establish a ring of security around the convoy and take a rest break. If a vehicle malfunctioned or had a flat tire, we'd leave a small group of people there to assist our mechanics. We always had mechanics and tow vehicles with us on convoys. They would stay behind and fix the vehicle and catch up with the convoy later.

There were tense moments, especially when we had to go through the villages. Early in the war, before civilians fled, the villages were crowded, and many of the people were furious with our presence and our huge convoys disrupting their lives. One of these incidents is still fresh in my mind because it was my scariest moment in transportation.

We were rolling slowly through a village, and suddenly the narrow street was packed with people, angry and screaming. They were trying to halt our convoy. We'd been taught that when people try to stop a convoy, you just keep rolling forward. Stopping could be deadly.

I was in the lead Humvee. Suddenly, villagers started crawling onto our trucks, stealing whatever they could. Most of our materials were in containers, and those couldn't be breached. But a lot of the truck drivers would strap coolers or chairs on the back of their trucks, and those were easily picked off. The villagers were pulling off everything that wasn't tied down.

Iraqis were swarming around my Humvee. One young man jumped up and hung on to the side mirror, right next to my face. My driver and my gunner were with me in the vehicle, and they were terrified. *I* was terrified. I didn't know how this would end.

We had several trucks behind us, and young Iraqi men began lying down in front of them, trying to stop them in their tracks. It was one thing to have a hard-and-fast rule to "keep rolling," but it was another thing to actually contemplate rolling your trucks over prone bodies. The trucks were approaching the people lying down in the road, slowly, slowly, moving forward, as they knew they had to do—while recognizing the potential disaster in store if the villagers were run over. At the last minute, thank God, the villagers jumped up and out of the way.

So we kept moving. The man hanging on to my mirror was screaming at me, and he wouldn't let go. I carried an M-16 and an M-9 pistol, and I was trying to decide whether to take out my pistol and swat him on the forehead. But I just sat there and did nothing and let him hang on.

Finally, we were able to gain enough speed that the man hanging on to my mirror had to let go. My heart was pounding as the town disappeared behind us. But I was also aware of how lucky we'd been. What if the villagers had weapons? What if one of our soldiers had pulled a trigger?

That's where training kicks in, and the weeks that we spent in our mobilization station going through all those rehearsals mattered. We'd practiced what to do in an ambush. We'd practiced how to handle mobs. We'd practiced how to keep our cool in volatile situations. That training was invaluable. It was our lifeline. We knew that anything could happen, and we just did the best we could. Followed the standard operating procedures: stick together, take care of each other, stay calm.

I got a reputation for being a by-the-book commander, and the soldiers sometimes complained. For example, whenever we traveled, everyone was required to wear their Kevlar vests, long sleeves, and helmets—no exceptions. We saw other outfits that had looser discipline on the road because it was so hot. The soldiers would be in shorts and T-shirts with no helmets. But not our company.

If I caught soldiers not wearing their vests or helmets or proper uniforms, they'd be punished with latrine cleanup duty, which no one liked. But one time I got caught out of line myself. I'd jumped into my Humvee at Camp Arifjan, and I wasn't thinking about it, but my helmet was sitting beside me on the seat. As I drove past some of my troops, I waved to them, and they started wildly pointing at their heads. What? I didn't understand. Then I saw my helmet sitting there, and blurted out, "Oh, my gosh." I assigned myself a week of latrine duty, and I think my soldiers enjoyed that very much.

The soldiers didn't always like the rules, but they respected them. And every one of them came safely home.

In July, a columnist from the *Des Moines Register* named John Carlson arrived at our camp. John was very popular in Iowa, and he had a way of bringing the real story to people back home. He told me he got to Iraq by the seat of his pants. One day his bosses said, "Why don't you go to Iraq?" He just showed up there, unaccompanied, his only credential being a letter from the managing editor. He stayed at Arifjan and bummed rides to the battlefields in Iraq. He wasn't there to analyze war strategy, but to tell the human story of our soldiers in the field. As he explained it to me recently, "When people ask me to make some grand pronouncement about the war, I say, 'I saw it through a soda straw. I don't have any great opinions about the strategic successes or operations. I just knew where I was and where I wanted to go and what I saw.'"

John accompanied us on one of the more bizarre transportation jobs of our deployment—transporting Saddam Hussein's huge stash of American gold, which was retrieved by the military. We made several trips, loading pallets of gold bars on trailers and carrying them to Kuwait City airport, where they'd be dealt with by American Treasury officials. We estimated that we handled $2 billion in gold. Talk about precious cargo! It was probably our most nerve-racking mission.

*   *   *

During the first half of our deployment we were firing on all cylinders all the time. I think I averaged three hours sleep a night, and I lost a significant amount of weight. For me, it wasn't just the work, but also the stress of being responsible for my men and women. I'd worry when I was on a convoy, and I'd worry when I wasn't on a convoy, wondering if my soldiers were okay. Would I get everybody home again?

It was especially hard when we'd get word of an Iowa soldier who had died. Those combat units were our sister units. We knew those soldiers and had worked with them. It was rough, and I knew that many of my soldiers wished they were in Iraq full-time, in the thick of the action. A lot of guys really wanted to be action heroes. That would have been fine, but I now see that somebody was looking out for us from above. We were blessed to be in Kuwait instead.

But then the military started contracting with KBR for truck drivers. All of a sudden, we started seeing big, fancy eighteen-wheelers and red tractors coming into Kuwait. Our missions began being taken over by the contractors. Those drivers were earning $120,000 a year to our soldiers' $25,000, and my troops were disgruntled. More than the money, they were upset about losing the work—their mission.

At first, they didn't mind so much because they assumed it meant they'd just be going home. Some of them had deployed during Desert Storm and had gone home after four months, so they thought the same would happen to us now. But the current Army policy was 365 days BOG—boots on the ground. And we were going to stay put until our year was up.

Morale plummeted. One day soldiers thought they'd be seeing their families soon, and the next day they found out they had another seven months doing something they didn't come to do.

As a leader in that situation, it was my job to get them out of their slump. I gathered everyone together and in the strongest way possible said, "Listen, we're all in this together. And like it or not, this is the policy." Since KBR was taking over the driving, our new mission was camp security. Not a single one of my troops liked that. They were drivers and they wanted to be driving. It hurt to watch someone else come in and take over their job. But they were pros, and they just applied a stiff upper lip. We all did.

We were now assigned as basically a glorified force protection unit, managing security, screening the thousands of employees coming onto the post every day, and conducting roving patrols driving the perimeter of the camp. We'd also man the security towers, which meant sitting still for eight hours a day. I have to say, the mood was pretty glum. Every day I heard people complain, "I want to be driving . . . I want to be on the road." But we just had to suck it up.

After several weeks, the soldiers began to see an upside to our new role. No longer were we being called out in the middle of the night. The shifts were regular. There was time to do laundry or visit the PX, or grab a slice of pizza at one of the little pop-up restaurants on the base, or even catch an occasional movie. Life was a bit more normal, if you could call it that. It was only after they'd stopped driving that people realized how much pressure they'd been under and how tired they were from those sixteen- to twenty-hour days.

There were lighter moments on security patrol. Outside the camp, local Bedouins were herding sheep and camels, and sometimes the animals would stray over the berm into the camp. Our roving patrol would be called on to chase them back into the field. Some of the soldiers had an opportunity to test their camel-riding skills.

At the same time, communications with home were improving. Initially, we'd had one phone for thousands of soldiers. A plywood table was set up outside of the headquarters tent, with a push-button phone. Soldiers stood in line for hours to make a ten-minute call.

Things got easier when I was assigned to be mayor of Camp

Camden Yards. As mayor, I was responsible for all the logistics in the camp. But I also occupied the mayor's cell tent, and there were phones in the tent. My soldiers could stop by and make a call. Morale improved.

Being able to call home was priceless, but it was also more complicated than it was often portrayed in the media. We didn't have Internet access for video chats. Making a call involved connecting to a post in the United States that would then have to make a connection with the family—all paid for by long-distance phone cards. Technology was rudimentary.

When I wanted to call home, I would call Offutt Air Force Base, which is in Bellevue, Nebraska, near Omaha. An operator would connect me to Gail and Libby in Red Oak. I would hear my little girl's voice faintly across the line. Those calls were usually rushed and quite unsatisfying, especially for those of us with young children. Anyone who has ever tried to have a phone conversation with a three-year-old knows what I'm talking about.

Being a woman in a war zone was both gratifying and challenging. For the most part I avoided problems—and my own troops were very respectful. But I did encounter sexual harassment. My company was freestanding. I didn't have a battalion commander, and we were attached to the area support group. I'd go to their briefings. A commander from another battalion would sit in those meetings and wink at me and give me suggestive looks. It was annoying, but no big deal. After the meetings, though, he'd catch up with me and start a very insistent pitch.

"I want to take you out to Kuwait City," he'd say. "I'll apply for the passes. It'll be fun." I was embarrassed for him, and I turned him down, but he'd keep it up. "Come back to my tent with me," he urged after one meeting. "I've got chocolate fudge from the States. I've got wine."

Wine? I just stared at him. We weren't allowed to have alcohol in a combat theater. It was general order number one. And he was a battalion commander! I don't know if he actually had wine, but the overture was creepy. I tried to keep an even tone when I blew him off. I thought a lot about what I should do. I had no superior to go to, so I had to handle it on my own. I had to use my wits.

My first sergeant did not appreciate the way I was being treated, and he stepped in to help me out. If he saw me with the commander, he'd intervene, coming over with an urgent need—"Ma'am, we've got to get back to the company area." And he'd literally pull me away from the guy. I realized that even though I was a commander, I was vulnerable just for being a woman, and that infuriated me. What right did some commander have to take advantage of his rank to harass me?

And how could we expect the regular troops to respect their female colleagues if their commanders wouldn't do it? Our military discipline held us together, and when that foundation cracked, it could be very destructive. We had a lot of infantrymen rotating back from combat, and there was a testosterone-heavy atmosphere around them. I had a few run-ins. In particular, there was a group of soldiers who would hang out around the female shower trailer, taking pictures every time the door opened. When I caught sight of them I marched over and shouted, "Hey! Put your phones away. Get out of here. This is the female area." I outranked them all, but they refused to leave. They just ignored me.

I was in a rage. I left and got one of my maintenance sergeants, a big, burly guy, and brought him back with me.

"You leave or I'm going to make you leave," he boomed at them, and they scurried away.

I was angry and embarrassed by the whole incident. Sure, I was a small woman, but I was also a captain, and the idea that soldiers would ignore my orders infuriated me. Fortunately, I never had this problem with my own men. They knew I would do anything for them, and they'd do the same for me.

Finally, it was time to ship back home, and we went as a unit. Our fly-out date was originally scheduled for March 30, 2004, and as with any movement, the date kept getting shifted. We finally arrived in the United States in the early part of April. We'd spent our final few days packing duffels and footlockers, and distributing home-made furniture we no longer needed to other units. We flew out of Kuwait City International Airport, cheering as we left the ground. The airport was crowded with arriving troops, and they were in our silent prayers as we left. After refueling in Ireland, we headed for Bangor, Maine. Bangor was the place where most of the troops made their first stop on returning. The Maine Troop Greeters, an organiza-tion of veterans and supporters, were there to meet us, as they would be for future returnees. (Since 2003, they have greeted more than 1.5 million returning soldiers.) The greeters show up any time of the day or night, whatever the weather. As we deplaned, they waved American flags, shook our hands, and said, "Thank you for your ser-vice." We couldn't have asked for a better welcome, and I think most of us had tears in our eyes.

Our next stop was back to Fort McCoy, where we demobi-lized. They did medical screenings and debriefings and updated all of our records. Then we split into three separate groups going to welcome-home ceremonies at the three different armories we'd come from—Perry, Audubon, and Red Oak. I made sure that I or my first sergeant was present at all three ceremonies. I went to Perry, he went to Audubon, and finally I flew a Black Hawk helicopter back to Red Oak for the last ceremony at home.

Gail and Libby met me there, and we were all so overwhelmed with joy. I couldn't stop hugging Libby, who had grown so much in the year I'd been gone. She was four now. Our helicopter had arrived before the bus carrying my soldiers, but they finally got there, and we had a beautiful ceremony in the Red Oak High School gym. I was so proud of the men and women I had served with, so inspired by their discipline and work ethic—and so grateful to be standing with them in safety. Still it was bittersweet, knowing that so many others, including from the Iowa National Guard, were still engaged in the fight. There was not a dry eye as the Red Oak soldiers were welcomed home.

When it was all over, the tiredness set in. The first thing I wanted to do was drop my stuff at home, take a long, luxurious shower, and then head for Pizza Hut. I had been craving Pizza Hut pizza for a long time.

Of course, it was something of a culture shock to be back home. I found myself looking around the house and thinking, "Why do we have so much stuff? We don't need all this stuff." After existing with a footlocker and a couple of duffel bags, it felt like everything else was so much waste. I'd never been one to care about having a lot of stuff anyway. When you move around in the military, you learn to embrace minimalism. I still do.

In the months after returning, I had plenty of opportunities to contemplate the everyday courage I had witnessed from my National Guard company in Kuwait. Sad to say, there was a real sense of hierarchy in the minds of some combat soldiers, and a lack of respect for the support units like ours. It didn't help that as a woman, and a truck driver, I came home to people thinking I'd never left the comfort of my base. I was a combat veteran, but some people didn't see me that way. I was asked to give a speech at a Memorial Day event in Red Oak, shortly after returning home. I was sitting next to a member of the Women's Auxiliary for the local VFW. She kept telling me I should join the auxiliary, that it would be great to have a young person. I finally looked at her and said, "Well, I think I'll join the VFW." Her face screwed up in the same way people still do when I tell them my war stories and she said: "You can't do that. The VFW is only for men."

I was used to it, to be honest. We'd even had that attitude from some of the infantry units coming through our camp—like, "We're all that, and a bag of chips." But my soldiers worked really hard, and I was offended when they were diminished. Yes, we had a different mission, but without us, the infantry couldn't survive. They couldn't haul all the ammunition and water and food they needed on their backs.

At Camp Arifjan, we'd had a lot of units cycling back for medical emergencies and the like. They'd wait for flights back to the States. And I remember a soldier coming into the headquarters one day. At the time, we had a soft-serve ice cream machine in one of the dining facilities. As you can imagine, it was very popular. But this guy was infuriated. He said to me, "You guys shouldn't have ice cream because we don't have ice cream in Iraq—and *we're* fighting."

I guess there will always be those who think they're better because of their branch designation. But I prefer to think that we're all in this together, and we share the same basic goal: to defend America to the best of our ability, and to survive.

Much later, when I was running for the U.S. Senate, the question of whether or not I was a combat veteran was raised again. It was an old, useless argument by that point. I am a combat veteran because I served in a combat zone doing combat missions. I had the God-blessed fortune to not be ambushed or hit by an IED. But I very well could have been, and I like to think that my function ultimately protected other soldiers from attack as well.

When the criticisms came out in the campaign, my soldiers were very upset about it. It wasn't just an attack on me, but on them as well. One of my soldiers was a woman in Audubon who had been deployed with a man who would become her husband. She was furious. She had been a truck driver who risked her life on those dangerous missions. They'd risked their lives for our country. I guess it angered all of us. I understand that it was mostly a political ploy directed at me, but my soldiers felt as if it was an attempt to deny their courage and contribution. We didn't wear infantry patches, but we wore our transportation patches proudly.

John Carlson, our intrepid Iowa journalist, who spent time with National Guard divisions in Iraq, told me for this book just how much the Army relied on the National Guard. He recounted how one Marine commander, who had Iowa National Guard troops working under him, and called them "my boys," described the treacherous task of road clearing in one of the worst areas in Iraq, and told Carlson, "Man, it was a sad day for me when those Iowa National Guard soldiers left."

On another occasion, when Carlson told a soldier from the 3rd Infantry Division that he was writing about the Iowa National Guard, "the soldier grabbed me by the shirt and said, 'I want you to tell those Iowa National Guardsmen something for me. You tell them, thank you. I get to go home because of them.'

"It gave me goose bumps," John said.

Reflecting on his experience, John noted, "I thought I knew what it meant to be afraid. I didn't know what it meant to be afraid. I found out when I was fifty-five years old what it meant to really be afraid." On one of his forays with a National Guard battalion, he was at a camp where insurgents would target the mess hall with mortars every night. There were guys and gals who would not go to the evening meal because they knew it was a target. John was with a National Guard battalion in the mess hall one night, "and there was this horrendous explosion. Everybody just froze and I started to get the hell out of there." A guardsman sitting next to him grabbed his arm and said, "Just sit still. Where are you going to go? Just sit still and eat your meat loaf." A young man was killed outside the mess hall, only about thirty feet away, in the direction John had been heading.

As an aside, when John retired from the *Des Moines Register* in 2018, Major General Timothy Orr of the Iowa National Guard presented him with the Commander's Award for Public Service. We were all appreciative of the way he told the people back home what we were about, even as he risked his life to report about our service.

You can't do deployment into a war zone without being changed in some way. Military service is a very intense community—it's why we call each other brothers and sisters. And when the family breaks up and everyone goes their separate ways, it can be a shock to the system. It's much harder for Reserve and National Guard units because we get back to the States and we all go to our different communities. We're not with our unit, and we're not able to reflect on those shared experiences. We're returning to civilian jobs and back with our families, who may or may not understand what has transpired. Suddenly, the men and women who stood by us are no longer there. In active-duty units, by contrast, they all return to the same place that they came from. The next week they can go back to work and be with the same people they'd deployed with. That wasn't true for the Guard and Reserve.

You would think that being married to a military man, I would have had greater support at home. However, it was just the opposite. Gail understood the military, but he never really understood my experience. When I tried to share my deployment stories, he would quickly interrupt to recount stories of his own. So, like many of the men and women who served with me and in other companies, I struggled with a sense of isolation and a feeling that our families and friends just didn't understand. Soldiers need to talk, to unpack their experiences, but often they don't have that opportunity.

It was still in the early period of awareness about PTSD and about the needs of returning soldiers. In those years, we were pretty much left on our own to deal with any emotional issues. The mental health screenings were perfunctory. I made a vow to myself that I would try to find ways to support my men and women at home, as I had done in the field. I didn't know yet that this support would come from the path of government service.

COMMITMENT

*After so many years in the military, the call of public service in govern-
ment seemed a natural next step. When I look back on my time in state
government, first as the auditor of Montgomery County, and then as a
member of the state senate in Iowa, I can see how much I applied the
lessons of military discipline to my work. I felt proud to work on behalf
of Iowans, to fight their battles. There's a reason we call the job "public
service." We are servants of the people. We're not ruling the roost, we're
responding to the need. Our commitment means not standing on a pedes-
tal but being out among our constituents. I came to see government work
as a calling, more than just a job or a temporary elected position. Like my
National Guard service, it was an expression of patriotic duty.*

Chapter Five

THE CALLING

Politics had never been much on my radar growing up. My family voted Republican but wasn't particularly political. Before my deployment, I'd worked in two part-time positions in the county—zoning administrator and emergency management coordinator. The latter was a post-9/11 job. Before the terrorist attacks, we'd had no budget for emergency management. But those jobs weren't really political. Only after I moved back to Red Oak had I become nominally involved with the county GOP and in government.

Unknown to me, as I sweltered in the desert heat, the local Republican Party was setting the stage for my political entry. During my last few months overseas, they approached Gail and my mother with a question: Did they think I would consider running for county auditor when I returned home? Naturally, both of them thought I'd be a great candidate, but they didn't presume to speak for me. No one had ever heard me express an interest in political office.

This was an urgent matter for the party, because the auditor's office was a hotbed of controversy and disarray at the time. Most people don't understand what an auditor does, and might be surprised to learn just how influential the office is. The auditor sits at the center of county operations, basically keeping the county's books.

She is instrumental in preparing the budget, scheduling public hearings, and paying the bills. She is the commissioner of elections, and responsible for real estate transfers. Usually, if a job doesn't fit into another department—such as HR—it lands in the auditor's lap. It's a very busy office; the auditor interacts with citizens in a very intimate way—often when they are most vulnerable. Trust is important.

But Connie Magneson, who had been our auditor for twenty-four years, was tearing the county apart. We'd all read with shock about an argument at a budget meeting when she'd been accused of punching our female county supervisor. She was arrested for that, and while she was acquitted, it definitely left a bad taste. It wasn't just that incident, though. It seemed that Magneson preferred conflict over conciliation, an odd manner for an auditor. Her office was toxic. People at the courthouse said they kept their doors shut to avoid interaction with her. The county insurance representative reported that an after-hours meeting with her had turned into a fit of rage. He said, "After that point I swore I would never, ever go back into the courthouse after hours or without witnesses."

Nevertheless, Magneson had impressive longevity in the job. People were reluctant to run against her because they didn't want to get drawn into the fray, and because her experience counted for a lot. But for me, it was heartbreaking to see my community in so much turmoil. When I was approached while still in Kuwait, I agreed to consider it after I finished my deployment. But I had no idea how to run for office. I'd never even worked on a campaign.

I called my friend Mike St. Clair, who had been a classmate at Iowa State and who was very active in Iowa politics.

"Can you tell me how to run for county office?" I asked.

"I can do better than that," he said. "I can introduce you to someone who's been there. I know just the person."

That's how I first connected with Kim Reynolds, who would

become my mentor and close friend, and in many ways my ideal for public service. Kim, who was then serving as the Clarke County treasurer, began exchanging emails with me, and each one began with enthusiasm: "I'm so excited you're considering running," she'd write. "Now, here's what you have to do." Kim also spoke about the higher goals of service—the collaboration and teamwork that made a county run. Well, I knew a lot about collaboration and teamwork! I was living it every day in Kuwait.

By the time I returned to Iowa in April 2004, I was ready to run. Magneson's campaign immediately tried to disqualify me, announcing, "You can't run for a partisan office while you're on active duty." That was not true, as it was allowed with permission from the chain of command. I gathered all the necessary paperwork and stood firm. If I was worried that the voters wouldn't like having an auditor who had to take off occasionally for National Guard drill and service, I needn't have been. People liked that I was a soldier, and the Iowa values that went into being one weren't lost on them.

The campaign itself was nasty—a real introduction to gutter-style politics. Magneson's supporters were disruptive and angry, shouting me down at every event. When we scheduled a public debate, Magneson didn't even show up. She was trying to send a message that I didn't matter enough to stand next to on a stage or talk to, but I hoped her absence would reveal the truth of her character. During the muddiest moments of the campaign, I'd say to Gail, "I hope I know what I'm doing," but I always had faith in the voters. I thought our county deserved better than this ugliness. I'd just returned from a highly disciplined, supportive service environment, and I thought that's the way government should be run, too. Thankfully, the people agreed. I won by an overwhelming margin, and in 2005 I started my new day job in Red Oak.

The auditor's office is in the beautiful, historic Red Oak courthouse. It's a stunning three-story structure of brick and limestone, with elegant sculpting and a tall clock tower. The courthouse is the pride of Montgomery County, and I rarely went inside without pausing to admire this fine structure, so unique in our plain hometown.

But once there, I had a lot of cleanup to do. Magneson's staff had quit, and at first it was just me and Ted Schoonover, the deputy auditor I'd hired, who was retired military—he'd served in the 1168th as a support person back home. It shouldn't have surprised me that someone had created mischief, emptying the Rolodexes, leaving only blank cards, and dumping all the keys into a drawer unlabeled. Fearing sabotage, the computer company responsible for programming county records had gone into the system remotely after the election and backed up all the records. It was that bad.

My first task was to break down walls—literally. Magneson had separated her office from the main auditor's office with a sliding door secured by dead bolts. A bit paranoid, she'd had all the courthouse security cameras in there, with monitors on the wall so she could watch who was coming in and out of the courthouse from her desk. So, the first thing I did was move my desk back out into the main area. I was directly accountable to the people, and I was meeting them when they came into the office, I wasn't hiding away. If a citizen came in, I'd go to the counter and talk to them. My job wasn't high and mighty. It epitomized grassroots service.

During my first week, an elderly farmer came into the office and asked me to step outside into the lobby area. He was crying. He said he'd had a run-in with Magneson years earlier and "I swore I would never step foot in this courthouse again. Now that she's gone I can come back in." Seeing this proud man cry made a big impact on me. I still think of him sometimes; he symbolizes the commitment we must have in office to care in a personal way about those we serve.

We were a tight collaborative band in that office, and I was motivated to bring the same spirit to all the other offices. I started doing monthly department head meetings, and that way the department heads could get together and talk about what was going on. Through those meetings, we were all educated about the full scope of county business and weren't just operating in our own silos. Other department heads, who had previously avoided the auditor's office, fearing "the wrath of Connie," now became our partners and friends.

In a moving way, the war followed me home and into the auditor's office. One day Ted and I were meeting with Jerry Hansen, our county's veterans affairs director, who had an office upstairs. I knew Jerry pretty well, as he'd been my recruiter when I joined the National Guard.

A young veteran happened to stop by the office to say hello. In our small world, I immediately recognized him because I'd deployed with his brother. It was obvious that he was very troubled. I asked him to come in and sit down, and Ted, Jerry, and I began to talk to him. By the grace of God, the three of us were in the office that day, because this kid was about to combust with frustration.

Struggling with his emotions, he told us that he felt as if he had nowhere to go. His wife had lost patience with him. She didn't understand why he felt so unhappy—why he wasn't glad to be home. There in my office, we comforted him as only those who understood him really could. "All of us have been in your place," I reassured him. "We understand what you're going through, and we're here for you if you ever need to talk."

Jerry was able to give him practical ideas for what he could do next, and connected him to counseling services. He emphasized that there was no shame in being in a vulnerable position. Seeking help takes courage. When the young man left, feeling a little steadier, Ted, Jerry, and I looked at each other and shook our heads. "I'm glad we were here for that," Jerry said quietly. The experience left me think-

ing about how taking care of our own went above and beyond the
formal avenues of my new nine-to-five. We all wanted to be helpful
whenever we could be.

The war would come home to me in another dramatic way during that time. It was Friday, and our "lunch bunch," a group from the
courthouse that got together weekly at the Chinese restaurant on
the square in Red Oak, was enjoying ourselves. Then my phone rang,
and it was a staff person at the Army National Guard. He said, "Joni,
there's been a death, and we need you to go make a notification."

Joseph Milledge, only twenty-three, had been killed by a road-
side bomb in Baghdad. He had a wife and a one-year-old son at Joint
Base Lewis-McChord in Washington State, who would be simultaneously notified, but I was tasked with notifying his mother, who
lived in Glenwood, about thirty minutes from Red Oak.

The person who would normally do that job was on vacation,
which is why it fell to me. Thankfully, my dress uniform was ready.
I called Ted, and with a shaking voice, asked him to cover for me at
the office that afternoon, because I'd received an urgent call from the
Guard. I could tell by Ted's solemn response that he just knew what
I would be doing. Those urgent calls didn't happen very often.

I went home and dressed in my uniform, then drove to Glenwood,
where I met Chaplain Seiloff, the state chaplain, at the McDonald's
attached to the gas station. He got in my car and we drove to the
home of Carla Milledge, the sergeant's mother.

When she opened the door, she knew immediately why I was
there—I think every military family knows what it means when an
officer in full dress uniform comes to their door. She began to crum-
ple in tears as I, fighting tears myself, recited the script of notification. We went inside with her, and in her living room, I sat and cried
with her. It was the hardest thing I'd ever done.

We talked and prayed with her, and told her that the Army would be following up, and that they would assign a benefits person to her. We talked about her daughter-in-law and grandson in Washington, and assured her that they were being notified at that time. She cried and started showing me pictures of her son as a little boy. She grieved for her grandson whose daddy wouldn't be coming home.

By the time we made our way out, neighbors had gathered on the street in front of the house. They'd seen us arrive, and they knew, too. They crowded around, asking us questions, but I had to tell them firmly, "I'm sorry, we can't speak to you. You can visit with the family."

I drove the chaplain back to his car, and he could tell I was devastated. "Joni," he said, "I've done many of these notifications. I was really moved by the way you sat and cried with that mother, as a mother yourself, and that you took the time to look at her pictures. I'm glad you were with me today." I guess he was trying to make me feel better, but that day, and his reassuring words, would be stamped on my mind forever.

I won reelection to the office of auditor after four years, and toward the end of that term people started talking to me about running for higher office. Jeff Angelo, our district's state senator, called me one day to say he planned to step down and he thought I should run for his seat in the next election. I was intrigued by the possibility and called Mike St. Clair. "Do it," he urged.

"I don't know," I hedged. "The timing isn't great. Libby's in elementary school now, and I should stick closer to home."

"You don't want to regret missing out on this opportunity," he said. "The upside for Libby will be seeing her mother pursue public service in this way."

I didn't tell Mike—or anyone else—that my reluctance was also due to a personal crisis at home that had shaken me to the core.

* * *

The truth is, my marriage was imploding at that point. Our life together had been so good, especially in the early years, but that had started to change once Gail retired from the military and I took office. I think now that in the good years Gail was happy because he was the center of attention. He was the sergeant major and everything revolved around him. Once he was a civilian—Libby's dad or Joni's husband—he started to get restless and look for ways to be the center of attention again. Which he could be with another woman.

For a long time, I didn't notice anything amiss. I had my nose to the grindstone with my auditor's job. Gail was working for US Bank as the branch manager, and then he took a promotion to work in commercial lending. He picked up some additional duties over in the Council Bluffs branch, about an hour away from Red Oak, and commuted back and forth twice a week between the two branches. He'd often complain about the commute and his salary, and one day he just quit his job. He then took a third shift job at Pella windows down in Shenandoah, which didn't make sense to me. Now, not only was he commuting every day, but it was an overnight job.

I didn't understand his rationale, but I figured he was still finding himself after a long career in the military. So, I tried to be supportive and didn't worry too much. I was relieved when a second-shift job opened up in Red Oak, but it would mean an adjustment. Gail's hours were three to eleven, and we wouldn't see as much of each other. He'd have a lot of free time during the day while I was at work that he'd have to fill somehow. Maybe he could volunteer or help out at the school.

That was when Gail developed a close relationship with another woman, one of Libby's former babysitters, who now ran a day care center out of her home. She also worked for a philanthropic community organization, and that's where Gail reconnected with her.

Without my knowledge, the relationship quickly developed into more than a casual friendship. While I was at the courthouse every day, Gail was hanging out with her. One day, my sister-in-law went into labor, and I called Gail. I could hear the voices and laughter of children in the background.

"Gail, where are you?" I asked.

"I'm at the day care center," he said.

That was odd, but I wasn't suspicious. Just puzzled. I even tried to put a positive spin on it—maybe he was helping out. But soon I realized that he was spending a *lot* of time with this woman, and not just during the day.

The real wake-up call came when I found out that on the weekends I was away drilling with the National Guard, Gail would leave Libby with my mom at night and go to a bar with the woman. I exploded. "Our daughter is with my mother and you're out drinking with another woman!" I shouted. "How is that right?"

I wasn't a naïve person. I thought it looked like an affair. But Gail was smooth at diverting. "She's just a friend," he insisted. "Are you saying men and women can't be friends?" That gave me pause, because obviously I had male friends from the Guard and from work, and we all socialized and went out as a group. But I wondered, if she was just a friend, why didn't Gail invite her to our house for our gatherings? He saw her only privately.

It was true that I wasn't particularly adept at filling Gail's insatiable need for adoration. If we were out with a group of friends, and the guys started kidding Gail about his manhood—the stupid kind of ribbing men do—he'd blow up at me when we got home: "Why didn't you stick up for me?" It was exhausting. You couldn't convince Gail that people said things in jest. He thought his manhood was being questioned at every turn. He was a very high-strung person to be around. And his "friendship" with the local woman was really starting to get to me.

I confided in a close friend, but outwardly I held it all in, feeling more stressed each day. Late one night I confronted him. "I want you to stop seeing her," I said.

I expected to have a conversation about it, but Gail flat-out said, "I'm not going to give her up."

"But you're just friends?"

"Yes."

Right—friends who went out all night when his wife was away on National Guard duty. If I had done something like that, he would've hit the roof. Why couldn't he see how inappropriate it was? He dismissed my concerns without a thought. "There's nothing wrong here," he insisted.

It infuriated me that he could say such a thing—that he could be so placid in the face of a situation that was causing me so much pain. We were shouting back and forth. "You have to give her up," I declared, frantically issuing ultimatums. Angry, Gail jumped up and stormed out of the room, with me following him down the wooden stairs to the main floor. There was a landing near the bottom, with an old piano bench and some plants. It split off down more stairs to the living room on one side and the kitchen on the other.

I was behind Gail on the stairs, and suddenly he turned around and grabbed me by the neck with one hand and threw me down on the landing. It all happened so fast that I had no time to react. As I tried to get up, Gail put both of his hands on my neck and started pounding my head onto the floor. His anger and strength were too much for me. Dizzy and caught off guard, I was unable to fight. My throat was closed and I couldn't scream. I honest to God thought he was going to kill me. My only thought was "I am going to die." Finally, he let go and walked off. I lay there panting, flushed and in pain as my circulation came back and my heart stopped pounding. Finally, after many minutes, I slowly pulled myself to a sitting posi-

My family's farm in Stanton, Iowa. My dad took over the farm from his father, and he and my mom raised us kids there. We all worked hard on the farm, but I still think of my childhood as idyllic. *Culver family album*

This drawing was done by Red Oak artist Carroll Danbom. *Carroll Danbom Fine Art*

The Culver kids: (l-r) Julie, Joni, and baby Wade. *Culver family album*

I started wearing glasses in the fourth grade. They were nearly as big as my face, but at least I could see again. *Culver family album*

The Santa Lucia festival was a high point of every year in Stanton. Julie (right), Wade, and I dressed in the traditional costumes. *Culver family album*

Choosing the military was life-changing for me. For twenty-three years, first in the Army Reserves and then in the National Guard, I learned how to be a leader. I retired in 2015, my first year in the U.S. Senate. *Culver family album*

My parents, Dick and Marilyn Culver, on my wedding day. *Culver family album*

My wedding to Gail Ernst came during the summer floods of 1993. But the sun broke through during the ceremony. *Culver family album*

At Camp Wolf, the massive staging area for the Iraq War, the 1168th Transportation Company, under my command, was housed in tents. *Ernst personal album*

Libby was the light of our lives. The hardest thing about military service overseas was being away from my daughter for a year. *Ernst personal album*

During our first six months, the 1168th drove 402 supply convoys in theater, delivering 10.5 million tons of equipment and supplies. *Ernst personal album*

On my campaign bus, dubbed the Squeal Mobile, I traveled to every county in the state. *Charlie Neibergall/Associated Press*

On election night, November 14, 2014, I promised Iowans that I would make their voices heard in D.C. *Charlie Neibergall/Associated Press*

Occasionally, in Washington, the best way to start the day is with a ruck march—a military-style hike carrying heavy backpacks. I'll invite my staff to join me for a vigorous bonding exercise. *Ernst personal album*

Perched on a stool, I take questions from Iowans at town hall meetings across the state. It's the best way to learn what's on people's minds. *Ernst staff photo*

At the Iowa State Fair, I enjoy pitching in at the Pork Booth. Pork belly on a stick is a crowd favorite. *Ernst staff photo*

Before a Senate Armed Services Committee Hearing in January 2020 on upcoming defense programs, I take time to speak informally with Admiral Craig S. Faller, commander of the U.S. Southern Command, and Army General Stephen J. Townsend, commander of the U.S. Africa Command. *Bill Clark/Associated Press*

For my annual Roast 'n' Ride event, I jump on my Harley and lead hundreds of cyclists from Des Moines to Boone for a big family pig roast. In 2019, I announced my reelection candidacy there. *Ernst staff photo*

Every year, I make it a point to visit all ninety-nine counties in Iowa and meet people where they live and work. An early morning visit to The Bakery Unlimited in Winterset was a hands-on event. *Ernst staff photo*

Iowa senior senator Chuck Grassley and I surveyed the damage by air following the severe spring 2019 Missouri River floods. *Nati Harnik/ Associated Press*

On a congressional delegation to Kuwait and Afghanistan, the week before Thanksgiving 2019, I was especially delighted to talk to the brave women soldiers serving there. I was proud to meet these skilled, self-assured combat soldiers, filling jobs from which women were excluded during my service overseas. *Ernst staff photo*

Three generations of strong Iowa women. My mom, Libby, and me. *Ernst personal album*

tion, cradling my head. It took me a while to shake away the stars and get to my feet. My mind was in a fog, and I didn't know where Gail had gone. I still felt deeply afraid.

I slowly made my way up the stairs to Libby's room, clinging to the railing. I could hear her crying. When I entered her room, Gail was sitting next to her on the bed, his arm around her neck. "Let go of my daughter," I cried, my voice hoarse. Gail let go of Libby and stood up, trying to talk to me. I instantly grabbed her and pulled her out of the room and down the stairs, yelling for Gail to stay away from us. Grabbing jackets, I fled with my daughter to my car. With trembling hands, I started the ignition, while Libby cried, afraid and confused. I slowly drove to my mom's house a few blocks away.

It was the middle of the night, and my mom was quite alarmed to see our shaken figures on her doorstep. I didn't tell her what had happened, only that Gail and I had had a fight. Even in my desperate state, my face and neck red and my eyes swollen, I didn't want Mom to worry about me. She was obviously alarmed, but she didn't pry.

Soon after Libby went to bed, Gail showed up at the house, sobbing and knocking on the door. "Don't let him in," I cried. Mom wavered. "Maybe you should sit down and talk this through," she suggested. I kept saying no, and I guess Mom could see how anxious I was because she told Gail through the door, "Go home. You guys can talk about this another time." Then she turned to me. "Let's get some sleep."

The next day when I got to the courthouse, I went upstairs to talk to the victim's advocate. She was very kind. She sat me down and listened to my story with a look of genuine concern on her face. It was a relief to unburden myself, but I wasn't so sure about taking the matter further.

"This is domestic abuse, Joni," she said. "You can report it . . ."

"No," I said. "I don't want to report it." I couldn't imagine the consequences of going public in a town where everyone at the hospital knew me. Also, a part of me wondered about my own culpability. Had I pushed Gail too far? Was it partly my fault? My mind flashed to the night of my rape, and to my college experience working with abused women. We had always told them they weren't to blame for their abuse, but faced with the situation myself, I wasn't so sure.

She smiled encouragingly. "Okay, let's look at your physical condition. I'd like to go with you up to the hospital to make sure you don't have a concussion."

"Absolutely not." I shuddered. In this small town, it would have taken about five minutes for word to get out if I went to the hospital. So, we sat there and talked for a while, me crying and she giving me words of support. "I'm here if you want to talk, or you need anything," she said as I finally rose to leave.

I felt a little better, and also more determined. I wanted to file for divorce. I had to make sure this never happened to me again. I walked over to the county attorney's office to get advice. I knew him pretty well and trusted him. Standing in the doorway to his waiting room, which was packed with people, I was overcome with embarrassment. "Is he free?" I asked the receptionist.

"He's got folks in with him right now. Can I take a message?" she asked, assuming I was there on county business.

"I'll just catch up with him later," I said, trying to be casual.

I went back down to my office and focused on my work. I didn't know what I was going to do. Later in the day, Gail called, very upset. I wouldn't have described him as remorseful—knowing Gail, he thought what had happened was all my fault. But he wanted to talk, and he suggested counseling. "Come on, Joni, we can work on this."

I thought of all our years together, how happy we'd once been, and how we supported each other through our deployments. I thought of Libby and how she would be affected by a divorce. I thought of how I still loved Gail, in spite of everything, and how I didn't want a divorce. I thought of how saddened I'd been when my parents split. And finally, I thought we owed it to ourselves to try. So I agreed to counseling.

We picked a counselor at the military base in Offutt, an hour away. Before we went in, Gail said, "Don't talk about what happened that night." Not a great start, but I agreed. We did, however, talk about his relationship. Gail said he would stop seeing the other woman, although I later found out it was she who called it off.

We stayed together. To be honest, I was good at compartmentalizing. Professionally, I was a soldier, a leader of men and women. I was a public official, with important responsibilities managing my county. I was all of those things, and I wanted desperately to put on a brave face befitting my public image. But I was also a woman who could feel vulnerable at times, especially when it came to my marriage. I didn't want people to know because we have it drilled into ourselves that you're either weak or you're strong. There's no middle ground. There's no room for confusion. You're a happy family or you're not—and if you're not, it's all your fault. I wanted to succeed at my marriage, and I believed that I could if I put in enough effort.

Our relationship eventually stabilized, and Gail was never violent again. But we never fully regained the closeness that we'd had in the first years of our marriage. We put on a happy face in public, but privately our home life was often tense, as if we had struck a truce. Gail was a good father, and I took comfort in that. I vowed to keep the family together for Libby's sake, and prayed for the day when I could fully relax and be happy in my marriage again.

Thank God, I loved my work in service to the people of Montgomery County. And the next time I was approached about running for a state senate seat, I went for it. Kim Reynolds had run for and won the seat in 2008, but in November 2010 she was tapped for the position of lieutenant governor under the newly elected governor, Terry Branstad.

Branstad was an Iowa fixture. He'd first been elected governor back in 1983, when he was only thirty-six years old, and had served for sixteen years. Now, after more than a decade out of the governor's office, he had retaken the seat. The people of Iowa were glad to have him back. Raised on a farm, Branstad was a military veteran and a lawyer, and many Iowans had grown up under his leadership. When Kim told me about her new opportunity, I was very happy for her, and then she told me she wanted me to run in a special election to fill her vacancy.

I'd been the auditor for six years by then. Gail was working a steady daytime job at the airport. Libby was doing well. The time was right.

It was a big decision. Even though the state senate is only in session the first several months of the year, between January and April, and only between Monday and Thursday, it was still a two-hour drive to Des Moines and would mean I'd have to stay in an apartment there during session. I'd only be home for three-day weekends. Libby was used to my being away for National Guard drills and training, but this would be a more consistent absence. I sat Libby down and had a talk with her. "I'll only do this if it's okay with you," I told her. Libby was very mature for her age, and she'd already experienced and accepted my National Guard absences. But this was a big decision. "I think it will be all right," she said. I gently reminded her that she wouldn't see me for a few nights a week during session, but we'd have weekends together, and I'd be home most of the year. Also, Daddy would be there.

"Can I tell my friends?" she asked with a smile. I hugged her. "I'm proud of you," I said. My heart ached at the thought of being away from home. I hoped she would come to see me as a model for what was possible for women, and in the coming years that's what happened.

My lodging was also settled. Gail's daughter had recently married, and her husband had a condo in Des Moines sitting empty. He agreed to rent it to me.

All that was left to do was win the seat. It was November, and the special election would take place in two months, before Kim was sworn in as lieutenant governor. The new senator would join the 2011 session of the senate. I had to scramble to present myself to the Republican district convention, where I got the party's nod. For the next two months, I made my face known in every corner of our large district. District 48 encompassed eight counties—Adams, Clark, Decatur, Union, Montgomery, Taylor, Ringgold, and Page. Day after day, I drove through the sparse farmlands and small towns, knocking on doors. If possible, I wanted to shake every constituent's hand, and I had a lot of help from the party. I was amazed by the outpouring of support in my first campaign outside my home county. There were no polls, of course, and little money—I think we spent all of $26,000 on that campaign. I had no way to measure how I was doing, except for the warm handshakes and enthusiastic responses I received on the road. On election day, I won easily. I was sworn in a week after the other senators and started right away.

The first time I walked up to the Iowa statehouse to begin work, I had to stop and take in the spectacular sight. The Iowa statehouse in Des Moines is as majestic a setting as you'll find in any European capital. Sitting on top of a hill with a clear view of the city, it is a grand sandstone edifice with elaborate porticos of brick and limestone. The central dome is made of iron and brick, embossed with highlights of pure 23-carat gold. The dome had been regilded a decade before my arrival, and it was a pretty expensive process. But the capitol building gleamed in the sun.

The wood and marble interior is stunning, beginning with the entry under the massive dome, with large columns and a wide marble staircase rising above. Around the rotunda on a sweeping band above the columns are the words from Abraham Lincoln's Gettysburg Address: "This nation under God shall have a new birth of freedom that government of the people, by the people, for the people, shall not perish from the earth."

But for me, the most dramatic flourish was a huge mural that took up the full width of one wall. *Westward*, by Edwin Blashfield, was commissioned by the Iowa State Capitol Commission in 1904. It was in every way an ode to the heartland. As Blashfield described his masterpiece:

> The main idea of the picture is a symbolic presentation of the pioneers led by the spirits of Civilization and Enlightenment to the conquest by cultivation of the Great West. Considered pictorially, the canvas shows a "Prairie Schooner" drawn by oxen across the prairie. The family rides upon the wagon or walk at its side. Behind them and seen through the growth of stalks at the right come crowding the other pioneers and later men. In the air and before the wagon are floating four female figures; one holds the shield with the arms of the State of Iowa upon it; one holds a book symbolizing Enlightenment; two others carry a basket and scatter seeds which are symbolical of the change from wilderness to plowed fields and gardens that shall come over the prairie. Behind the wagon and also floating in the air, two female figures hold respectively a model of a stationary steam

engine and of an electric dynamo to suggest the forces which come with the later men. In the right hand corner of the picture, melons, pumpkins, etc. among which a farmer and a girl, suggest that here is the fringe of cultivation and the beginning of the prairie. At the left a buffalo skull further emphasizes this suggestion.

It always gave me a chill to look at the mural and feel the gravitas of Iowa's rich culture dramatized on the wall. It still does today.

It would be my first experience being part of a deliberative body. I was glad to have had the background of county government, serving at the most grassroots level, where the rubber meets the road. I'd loved working with the constituents and the citizens at that level, but actually diving into policy excited me in a different way. It was an opportunity to take what I had learned in the county and apply it through policy at the state level.

As elaborate as the design of our historic quarters was, the actual work area was bare-bones and pedestrian. I would soon find that state government is also very close to the earth. We got our hands dirty with real local issues—such as school bus routes, and how long children should be on buses, and the different issues that face urban versus rural school districts. We wrestled with how to improve agricultural prospects through conservation and water quality projects. We tackled the economy and sought ways to bring Iowa into a business- and taxpayer-friendly environment. We studied how to reduce unemployment while lifting commerce.

I was invigorated by the challenges of working on policy. I could see the ways we were making real, practical decisions that affected people's day-to-day lives and livelihoods. There was nothing abstract about our work. In every debate, I could imagine real families, and could structure policy in ways to help them. When I visited communities, and spoke to constituents, I kept them in mind and applied their stories to legislative solutions.

The senate was surprisingly informal. We didn't have allotments for offices in our districts. On many occasions, people came to my house in Red Oak for meetings. Sitting around the table, drinking coffee and problem solving, it seemed like the very definition of kitchen table government. Even at the capitol, we didn't have individual offices. We literally worked on the floor of the senate.

If you were in leadership, you had a workstation behind the floor, but it wasn't exactly private—just a cubicle in a room with other cubicles. The rest of us operated right on the floor of the senate. It seemed very basic at first, but I came to find it advantageous. I could look across the floor and see my colleagues right there—or walk across the floor to buttonhole them for impromptu discussions— "There's Joe Bolkcom from Iowa City, I need to talk to him about this aquaculture tax credit."

Along the outer walls were black leather–covered wooden benches, and a lot of huddles would take place there. There was one bench in particular that came to be known as "Joni's bench," because that's where I'd be if I was trying to work out a problem with another senator. It was hands-on government.

We talked to each other, Democrats and Republicans. Being in such close quarters forced us to have conversations with those we didn't necessarily agree with. We couldn't hide out in our offices because there weren't any offices. Each of us was allowed one clerk. We'd sit at small desks with our laptops, and the clerk would set a laptop on top of a file cabinet next to a desk, and do business that way. To support us on the issues, caucus staff would provide input on specialty areas like agriculture or human services, but that was it. We didn't have actual staff— just our clerk. We handled our own correspondence and scheduled our meetings. I answered my phone and made my own calls.

I spent as much time as possible out in my district, visiting the counties at least once a month. While the legislature was in session I would hold town hall meetings. Then, throughout the year, it was up to me to arrange attendance at Farm Bureau meetings, confer with bankers, and interact with chambers of commerce. As a senator, I often felt like a sole practitioner.

There was a lot of travel. My district with its eight counties was the largest geographical district in the state of Iowa. To get from point A in Montgomery County all the way over to point B in the southeastern part of my district was a two-and-a-half-hour drive.

Roby Smith, who represented Davenport and came from a highly populated district, used to joke with me about the difference between representing urban and rural areas. He said, "The other day I was at the furthest point away in my district and my wife called to say, 'Supper is ready.' I told her, 'I'll be there in five minutes.'"

The state senate is the place where we did the nitty-gritty business of the state, but that doesn't mean there weren't highly charged emotional moments over larger issues of morality and integrity. One of these came in my first year over the Stolen Valor Act. This was close to my heart.

The Stolen Valor Act, which was introduced by one of my Republican colleagues, was pretty basic. It would prohibit people from falsely claiming that they had earned awards and decorations that rightfully belonged to members of the military. Republicans were in the minority, and Senate Majority Leader Mike Gronstal of Council Bluffs was stalling on advancing the bill, based on vague ideas about free speech. Gronstal compared lying about military service to lying about your age or weight, and said it would criminalize kids who pinned on their fathers' military badges.

That was nonsense, and it really burned me. So I gave a floor speech and laid it all out. I was impassioned because this involved our military heroes. My anger showed. "We are calling this the Stolen Valor Act because that is exactly what we are attempting to stop—the theft of honor earned in wartime by everyday Iowans who went above and beyond the call of duty," I raged. "I understand that some of my colleagues from across the aisle are concerned that this act would infringe upon the right to free speech. I cannot begin to comprehend your hesitation in this specific instance. . . . I pray my colleagues on the other side of the aisle search deep within them and find the intestinal fortitude to demand that this bill come to the floor of the Senate for consideration."

And then I brought up Sergeant Joseph Milledge. Milledge had been weighing heavily on my mind ever since I had been assigned to give a death notification to his mother, and now he symbolized for me the honor we were trying to protect. "Sergeant Milledge paid for his posthumously awarded Purple Heart with his blood, and the blood of a comrade in arms," I said. "Let us not allow his Purple Heart to be cheapened by some Joe Schmoe on the street that tries to pass himself off as a hero to others to gain some personal advantage."

When I finished my speech, Gronstal made a beeline straight across the floor to me. He was mad! Steam was coming out of his ears. He got right up in my face, yelling and spraying spittle. "If you want to play politics, go ahead!" he screamed. "This is unconstitutional. You're just trying to score points."

A couple of my Republican colleagues were watching, thinking they might have to rush in to save me. But then they saw my face. I was totally calm, staring right at Gronstal without backing down. They said, "Whoa, Joni's got this."

I was bound and determined to move that bill. And it did move and was signed into law. I think the day I gave that speech was the day my colleagues realized I meant business.

In the state senate, I got a vivid sense of being the people's servant. None of us were in it for the glory—or the money, which was about $27,000 annually plus a few per diems and gas receipts. That pay didn't go far when you were renting lodgings in Des Moines. I guess that's why so many legislators were either retired or had separate businesses. It was a little trickier for me because my National Guard service made it hard to get an additional part-time job.

In fact, in my first year in office, I went almost directly from the statehouse to the flood zone after the end of the session. My National Guard unit was mobilized for the devastating Missouri River flood in the western part of the state. My role as a liaison officer in southwest Iowa kept me busy for several months. It was hard work, and the disaster was overwhelming for those communities. I viewed it as an extension of my legislative work, serving the people, especially in the worst times. In the quiet nights, bone weary, the damp grit in my boots and hair, and my eyes burning from the sights of devastation I'd seen, I was heartened by the way Iowans were once again coming together to help their neighbors—as we always had.

That fall I received a very surprising and gratifying call from Colonel Tim Rickert of the Guard. When I saw his number come up on my cell phone, I thought he was probably looking for a guest speaker, as it was right before Veterans Day. Instead, he said, "Joni, you've been selected for battalion command." I was so overcome, I almost burst into tears. A battalion command was beyond my aspirations. It was about as high as you could go and still work with soldiers. I would be responsible for one of the Combat Sustainment Support Battalions. Hundreds of soldiers would be under my direction.

Being a battalion commander gave me a way to express my commitment on a deeper level. I vowed to take care of my soldiers and encourage them in ways they might not have experienced before. I received stacks and stacks of promotion orders for my troops, and I didn't let my staff deliver them until I stuck a personal note on each one, thanking them for their service. When you serve, it's easy to see everyone as part of a whole—a means to an end. I wanted to make sure that my soldiers knew that someone recognized their sacrifices in an individualized way. And it really made a difference to the men and women under my command. It was important to them and their families that "the brass" appreciated their service.

Chapter Six

"MAKE 'EM SQUEAL"

I was in my second term in the state senate when the news broke that U.S. senator Tom Harkin, a Democrat who had represented Iowa in Washington for nearly thirty years, was not running for reelection in 2014. The announcement caught everybody by surprise.

In church one Sunday shortly after, I felt a nudge from behind. "Joni, you should run for that Senate seat," whispered Delane Hanson, a farmer and seed dealer who lived south of Stanton. I turned around and whispered back, "Thank you, Delane. That's very sweet of you." But I didn't take it seriously.

Other people around town mentioned it, but I brushed off their comments as the kind of thing "friends of Joni" would say. Then one day in the senate, as I was walking off the floor, a colleague pulled me aside. "You really should do this," he said. He had a lot of credibility, but I wasn't sure.

"I wonder if this is something I should consider," I said to Gail and Libby one evening. Gail shrugged. "If you want. You supported me through my active-duty service, so I'll do the same. It's up to you." He was sincere. Our marriage was doing better at the time, and I honestly felt that Gail was proud of me.

"I don't know," I said, looking at Libby. "Des Moines is one thing. Washington is a long way from Red Oak."

But what was really stopping me was the belief that this opportunity rightly belonged to Kim Reynolds, if she wanted it. I knew she was considering making a run.

One day while I was on the floor of the senate, Kim texted me. "Can you come down to my office when you're through?"

"Yep . . . I'll be down after the vote series," I texted back.

I knew Kim had just returned from Washington, where she'd met with the National Republican Senatorial Committee. I assumed they'd urged her to run. As I walked down to her office, I prepared myself for her announcement, and thought of ways I could help her campaign. I was going to tell her, "I'm ready to be volunteer number one."

When I walked into her office, Kim beamed at me, and she seemed extremely excited. We sat down and she got straight to the point. "Joni, I've decided not to run for the Senate. I'm going to run for reelection with Terry. I think you should run."

"What?" I hadn't expected that.

"You should run," she said again.

"Kim, oh my gosh, I just need to think a little bit more about it," I said. It was almost comical. Kim had flipped the script. I had been so focused on Kim's potential run that I'd stopped thinking of myself in that role.

"We'll help you," she assured me. In the coming days, I began to hear the same message from my colleagues. Nancy Boettger, a trusted colleague from western Iowa, who had been in the senate for eighteen years, promised all the help I needed. Nancy and I were prayer warriors together, participating in a weekly Bible study, so that help included prayers. Once again, as I had experienced so many times in my life, just when you think you're on your own, you have a whole army of people beside you.

When I finally made the decision to run, it was as if a great weight was lifted off my shoulders. With it came a strong resolve: I was going to outwork everybody, and I was going to win.

I formally announced my candidacy in July 2013, standing in front of the Montgomery County Courthouse in Red Oak, surrounded by friends and family. Then I embarked on a six-stop introduction tour. I spoke of Iowa values: "As a mother, soldier, and conservative, these Iowa values are what I hold dear. And they're threatened by the failed values of Washington."

So far in my political career, there hadn't been much press interest in me, but now there were usually at least a couple of reporters at my events. Across Iowa, there were hundreds of everyday working public servants who never generated a mention in the press. We like to imagine that ours is a citizen government, where ordinary farmers and soldiers and businesspeople can put down the tools of their trade and ascend to the representative pinnacle in Washington. We still hold a piece of that Frank Capra dream. But in our day the media can be scavengers of dirt and drama as much as tools of communication. I was ready for a rough ride. But I was cheered by the enthusiastic support of my local friends and family. My pastor confessed that although he was behind me all the way, his first thought when I announced my candidacy was that he'd have to find a new confirmation teacher at church. Although I could no longer commit to teaching, I vowed to stay as involved as possible in my congregation on my weekends home.

Two other Republicans had already announced their candidacies: attorney Matt Whitaker (who would later briefly serve as acting attorney general in the Trump administration) and former Grassley chief of staff David Young (who later became a congressman in Iowa's 3rd Congressional District). Others would jump in, including talk show host Sam Clovis and wealthy energy executive Mark Jacobs. I was the only woman.

Once I announced, I had to assemble a team, and that would mean hiring consultants who were expert at organization, publicity, and fund-raising. I got a lot of advice about this from more experienced people. One of these was David Polyansky, a former Marine who had served in Iraq, an advisor I felt comfortable with. In the beginning, it was just David and his business partner, Ashlee Rich Stephenson, and me.

We were on a shoestring budget, and nobody knew who the heck I was, which was a challenge. When I started making fund-raising calls with a list of potential donors, I was just a stranger calling. I spent long hours on the phone in my attic office in our old house in Red Oak. Most of the time, the response was, "Who are you again?" and, "What did you say you were running for?" I'd launch into my pitch, often to dead silence on the other end of the line. In the beginning, before we were able to hire a fund-raiser, it was just me.

I'd make detailed notes of all my calls. It was uncomfortable, but I was persistent. I found that it took an average of eight calls to get a yes. After hearing from me repeatedly, people would say, "I have to hand it to you. You don't give up. I'm going to give this time." Calling strangers to ask for money took a lot of nerve, and each time I started I had to give myself a little pep talk. It went against my upbringing, which taught me not to ask people for favors, to handle things on my own. Especially, to never ask for *money*! But that kind of rugged individualism wasn't going to get me elected.

It was a long primary race, and I had plenty of opportunities to go up against my opponents in forums and debates. I enjoyed that part of the campaign. It was also the most rigorous. In a debate, you had to be prepared to answer any question sent your way, and I was always determined to be the most prepared. I was already quite well versed in state issues, but now I had to know what was going on in the Obama administration and Congress—taxes, spending, agriculture, education, social issues, foreign affairs. The briefing book was pretty thick. I wasn't about to be the one who was stumped on the stage, or, God forbid, to make a gaffe that would follow me through the campaign. My advisors were also pushing me to have a signature issue that would define me and help me stand out.

My campaign had hired Todd Harris, a veteran Republican strategist, to help me hone my message. As we neared the final debate and the June primary, I needed a way to break through the crowded field. I was still struggling to become known by the voters against candidates with deeper pockets and better name recognition. How did I avoid becoming an also-ran?

Todd was looking for a more personal way of messaging. He sat down with me and said, "Just tell me about your childhood. Tell me about growing up on a farm." I described different farm chores, how we all pitched in during harvest, preparing meals for workers in the field. At the end, I added, "And we used to cut hogs, or castrate hogs."

Todd held up a hand to stop me. "What?"

I laughed. "It's true. You take the little boy piglets and you . . ."

"That's incredible," Todd said, and went home that night to search for a YouTube video of pig castration. He came back the next day and told me that he started the video, and then turned it off, feeling a little green. "I couldn't watch." I enjoyed his discomfort.

As we continued to brainstorm, Todd kept coming back to the hogs. He liked the images of life on the farm, and continued to be intrigued by the hog story. Finally, he snapped his fingers—an inspiration. "You want to cut pork in Washington, right? Let's make an ad about cutting pork and tie it in to your childhood castrating hogs."

"Well, I don't know," I said, ever cautious. "Do you really think castrating hogs is a good topic for an ad? I don't want people to laugh at me."

"Trust me," Todd said, grinning. And so I did.

Before cutting the ad, we tested it in a debate about the economy. I was standing on the stage with my four opponents. When it was my turn to state my views, I said, "Well, you know, I grew up castrating hogs, so I know how to cut pork." The audience, which was supposed to remain silent during the debate, burst into loud laughter.

"See," Todd told me after the debate. "People like it. Let's do the ad."

The ad, titled "Make 'em Squeal," showed me standing in front of hog pens. "I'm Joni Ernst. I grew up castrating hogs on an Iowa farm. So, when I get to Washington, I'll know how to cut pork"—and a hog squeals.

The day after the ad aired, I was walking into a library in Des Moines for an event when I got a text from the campaign: "Oh, man, Jimmy Fallon played your ad on the *Late Show*." Then, a second text: "Stephen Colbert talked about your ad on his show." I saw the clip and it made me laugh. Colbert, in his character as a conservative talk show host, said, "Joni, you had me at castration. Folks, it does not matter what else she stands for. I am pulling for her whole hog, or whatever is left of the hog when she's done with it." Other shows were running the ad, including *Good Morning America*. Overnight, I became the "Make 'em Squeal" lady—or as some people called me, "the pig lady."

Some donors were not happy. "Joni, that's disgusting," one said to me. But the grass roots loved it. It wasn't just the straight talk, it was the identification with life on the farm, and was representative of my desire to do something different in Washington—instead of being part of the problem, breaking down the bureaucracy that had for too long hurt Iowans. Many times, people came up to me at rallies and said, "I did that, too," and, "I still castrate hogs today." But it didn't just appeal to the hog castrators. The ad broke through the noise of the campaign and established me as a tough cost-cutter.

A second ad made the point in a different way. It showed me riding up on my Harley-Davidson with a voice-over reciting: "Joni Ernst, mom, farm girl, lieutenant colonel . . . [loading a gun] but there is more than just lipstick in her purse. [Aiming] Joni Ernst will take aim at wasteful spending and once she sets her sights on Obamacare, Joni's gonna unload". . . [fire]. Oh, and one more thing [bull's-eye target covered with hits]. Joni doesn't miss much."

Those two ads gave me instant national recognition, and established me as a strong, no-nonsense candidate. Virtually overnight, the poll numbers started to shift in my favor. But on the flip side, for the first time, my opponents were going on the attack against me. Mark Jacobs, who was self-funding his campaign and who had blanketed the airwaves and the Internet with his ads, put a statement on his website shortly before the primary, accusing me of being "AWOL" from the state legislature and missing some votes. It was very offensive to me because I felt it denigrated my National Guard service. In this I got unexpected support from none other than John McCain, who sent a statement to *The Des Moines Register*:

> It was bad enough that Mark Jacobs called Joni Ernst "AWOL" while she was on duty serving in the Iowa National Guard, but the fact that he has refused to remove this offensive term from his website is inexcusable. . . . The fact is that Joni Ernst has a 90 percent voting record, and I am proud to call her a fellow veteran of our armed forces. Mr. Jacobs should immediately take down his attack website, and apologize to Lt. Col. Ernst and all the men and women she serves with.

I was very touched by McCain's support, and by the way he helped turn a negative attack into a promotion for our National Guard. After that, Jacobs took the AWOL claim off his website.

The insult cut me because I saw myself as the opposite of disengaged. For my entire life I'd been learning the importance of hard work in every arena—from the farm to the military to political office. My parents had a principle that stuck with me: "If something needs doing, do it yourself. Get in there and pitch in." It offended me to be accused of slacking by people in pressed suits who'd never think of hauling themselves up onto a tractor.

I had been a long shot in the five-way race, and I felt confident I could outdo my opponents. But there was a catch. If the winning candidate didn't get at least 35 percent of the vote, the nominee would be picked by a statewide Republican convention. On primary day, I prevailed with 56 percent of the vote. There would be no convention.

It was a very emotional moment as I stood on the stage in a ballroom in Des Moines with my family gathered around me. There were tears in my eyes. "Whether you voted for me today or someone else, I promise you I will work every single day to earn your trust and support."

A month after my victory in the primary, I headed out for my annual two-week National Guard training—what my former opponent had called being "AWOL" from the senate. Before I left, I taped the Republican weekly radio address from the senate, explaining, "I'm recording this message a few days early, and by the time you hear this, I will be on active duty."

As battalion commander, I had all my units together at Fort McCoy, Wisconsin, my old stomping ground. This time there was a special experience in store for me.

One of the planned exercises was Taser training, which involved soldiers actually being tased. Beforehand, a sergeant first class in the military police who was up for reenlistment said, "The only way I'll reenlist is if I get to tase the battalion commander."

I said, "Okay, you can tase me as long as you'll be reenlisting." So I joined the company commander, who insisted on going first. We both thought it was good for the soldiers to see the leadership being tased. I figured that the young soldiers would realize that if the older lady could do it, so could they.

My campaign was a little freaked out when they learned I was going to be tased. I think they were worried that someone would take a video and it would be spread on the Internet. But I reassured them that no cell phones would be allowed.

There was a mattress covered with plastic sheeting on the floor, because some people lose bladder control. A soldier stood on each side of me, bracing me. When the current from the sergeant's Taser hit me, it was horrible. My muscles seized up and I stiffened. The soldiers grabbed my arms and laid me down on the floor until the electric shock passed. It only lasted about ten seconds but it felt like minutes. The soldiers kept saying, "Ma'am, it's almost over . . . It's almost over . . . five more seconds." And once it was over they dug out the prongs—one had gone into my back and one into my rear end—and I got up, feeling wobbly but intact. I felt proud as I shook hands with the newly reenlisted sergeant. I knew I was probably the only Senate candidate in 2014 to be tased.

Democratic candidate Bruce Braley waltzed into the general campaign as though he were the Chosen One. He'd always seen himself as Harkin's heir apparent, and I imagine he was delighted that I'd be his opponent because he didn't think much of me or my chances. A four-term congressman from eastern Iowa, Braley thought he had the election won before it started. He certainly had far more money than I had, and better name recognition in the state. But I saw his weaknesses. He had a trial lawyer's cockiness, and was prone to inadvertent displays of elitism. When the federal government had shut down in October 2013, he'd complained to a reporter about the hardship felt in the congressional gym: "There's no towel service, and so we're doing our own laundry down here." Of course, he was widely mocked for that statement, and I took particular pleasure in talking about how many loads of laundry I did a week, all while serving in the state senate, drilling for the National Guard, and raising my daughter. (Years later, when the Senate gym was affected the same way, I took the towels home and washed them myself. That's what real Iowans do—at least, Iowa women!)

Braley suffered from overconfidence, and while I was traveling to all ninety-nine counties, he wasn't seen much out among grass-roots voters. For me, that was the best part of the campaign. I had a bus, dubbed the Squeal Mobile, with my name and a little pig insignia against a backdrop of an American flag and a cornfield. On the back panel of the bus was a big map of Iowa, and at each stop people could sign the map with a Sharpie—"Good luck"... "Thanks for visiting." It was a lot of fun. People loved signing that map. Often, they'd videotape friends and family signing the bus. It made them feel like a part of our campaign.

Right out of the gate, Braley made a potentially fatal faux pas when he attacked Senator Grassley in a crude and insulting way. One thing most Iowans agree upon, regardless of party, is reverence for Grassley. Braley was speaking at a fund-raiser in Texas when he began to talk about dire consequences for the nation if there was a GOP takeover of the Senate, including the fact that Grassley, "an Iowa farmer who never went to law school," would become chairman of the Senate Judiciary Committee. There was his elitism showing again! After the video leaked out, he apologized profusely to Grassley, but the repercussions of the comment were felt throughout the campaign.

Senator Grassley was my greatest champion and guardian angel, along with his warm and supportive wife, Barbara. They showered me in support, treating me like a neighbor and a friend. If Grassley couldn't be at an event, Barbara Grassley would be there. Every chance he got, Grassley told people, "You've got to be supporting Joni Ernst. We need her." He was magnificent.

Walking by Grassley's side at the Iowa State Fair, I felt as if I were in the company of a rock star—but a rock star that ordinary people considered a friend. "Grassley! Grassley!" people shouted when they saw him. He'd stop every few feet to tell them, "I'd like to introduce you to someone. This is Joni Ernst, she's running for the Senate." It seemed as if he knew every single person by name.

The second day of the fair, as Braley and I stood side by side grilling pork in front of snapping photographers, Grassley went around to the tables and poured iced tea, happily chatting with constituents about farming, which is his favorite topic. Spotting reporters, he suggested that they visit the pig birthing barn if they wanted to learn something meaningful. I'm not sure any of them took him up on it.

I was fully aware that it wasn't just my election that was at stake. The *Senate* was at stake. Republicans were the minority party, which gave them little leverage with the Obama White House. We needed to gain at least six seats in 2014, and my seat was one of them. For this reason, my race got special attention from heavy-hitters in the party who came out to Iowa to campaign by my side—including Marco Rubio, Mitt Romney, Rand Paul, and Lindsey Graham, who said of me, "It would be nice to have somebody in the Senate who doesn't *talk* about boots on the ground, but has *had* her boots on the ground." (Of course, Braley had his own entourage of campaigners— the Clintons, Michelle Obama, and Elizabeth Warren.)

Braley and I had three debates. The first, sponsored by the *Des Moines Register*, was held at Simpson College in Indianola, and was televised. The minute Braley walked onto the stage, I could feel his arrogance, like he was wondering why he'd even had to bother to debate such a country bumpkin. He'd once referred to me as a "flash in the pan," and I knew he wished he could just wave his hand and send me on my way.

But as the debate went on, I saw that I could use Braley's dismissiveness to my advantage. I'd really hit the books in preparation for the debate, and it seemed to me that Braley hadn't bothered to prepare. He thought he could spew the usual boilerplate about right-wing tools of the one percent, but I didn't let him get away with it. When he wound up with an assault on the Koch brothers' funders, I came right back at him. "Congressman Braley, you're not running against these other people, you're running against me." Besides, I added, "You are being funded by Tom Steyer, who is a California billionaire extreme environmentalist."

And I did score a big hit toward the end of the debate. It is often true that who we are is exposed not by what we say about the issues but by how we behave away from the spotlight. Braley had demonstrated that perfectly in 2014 when he got into an ugly spat with a neighbor. The Braleys had a vacation lake house on Holiday Lake. Their next-door neighbor, Pauline Hampton, had chickens, and on a couple of occasions the chickens strayed into the Braley yard. One day Hampton showed up at the Braley household with a neighborly gift of a dozen eggs, only to be told that they didn't want her eggs and, in fact, had filed a formal complaint against her and her chickens, and hoped to have the chickens banned altogether.

She was obviously upset, but she did build a wire fence. The Braleys did not drop the complaint. When I'd heard about the incident, following Hampton's declaration that she was going to vote for me, I saw it as typical of Braley's sense of entitlement, and a clear violation of "Iowa nice."

In the debate, Braley was boasting about his ability to work across the aisle and compromise in a bipartisan way. When it was my chance to respond, I turned to him and said, "How can we expect you to work across the aisle when you can't even walk across your yard and work out an issue with chickens with your neighbor?" The audience laughed, and Braley looked furious. After the debate, he didn't even stick around for the media avail. He stormed out the back door. I think it rattled him that I wasn't a pushover.

I enjoyed the debates, and I was always prepared, practicing my answers with my family in the greenroom right up until the final minutes. I decided to just go out there and be myself, and then let the voters decide. Once I got on the stage, I wasn't nervous at all. I knew what I believed in and what I wanted to say.

Although I was running to become the first woman ever elected to Congress from Iowa, the Democrats didn't hesitate to play the woman card against me. Debbie Wasserman-Schultz, then the chair of the Democratic National Committee, called me "an onion of crazy—the more you peel back the layers, the more disturbing it is." Braley wasn't any less subtle. A campaign ad against me, featuring a chirping chicken, seemed to be trying to compare me to a "chick." The message: I was a *crazy chick*. Was that the best they could do?

Braley hit me hard on the abortion issue. I had always been open about being pro-life. It wasn't just a political position for me; it was a fundamental belief in the sanctity of life. It was a matter of conscience. But I wasn't the rabid pro-lifer Braley painted me as. I believed in exceptions, particularly for the life of the mother. And I was a great champion of birth control. During one debate, he accused me of secretly wanting to deny women birth control coverage. I fought back indignantly. "This is a ploy to scare women," I said.

"I will protect their right to birth control." Later, as a senator, I would put forward a bill that would allow women to buy birth control over-the-counter—an effort I'm still working on today, and one that I view as both pro-woman and pro-life.

One of the other issues that was discussed during my campaign was sexual assault and harassment in the military. This issue was personal for me. I'd had my fair share of harassment in the military, even after I became a commander. Fortunately, it never escalated and I was able to handle it on my own. But we know women get harassed regularly in the military, and they need to be protected by their comrades on the inside. When it's a matter of assault, it's a much graver matter. Those women deserve unbiased representation. I promised to be their advocate once I was elected—which I did; more about that later—but there wasn't a word from my opponent about it.

Braley's campaign tried to boast about being supportive of women while hypocritically dragging me down in sexist ways. His supporters followed suit. Near the end of the campaign, Senator Harkin, stumping for Braley, made the ultimate sexist comment. Speaking at a Democratic barbecue on October 26, Harkin was filmed saying, "There's sort of this sense that, 'Well, I hear so much about Joni Ernst. She is really attractive and she sounds nice.' Well, I got to thinking about that. I don't care if she's as good looking as Taylor Swift, or as nice as Mr. Rogers, but if she votes like Michele Bachmann, she's wrong for the state of Iowa."

Taylor Swift? I was insulted on two levels. One, the pure sexism of defining women candidates by their appearance and niceness. Two, the insinuation that I was unserious and didn't belong in the race.

Harkin offered a backhanded apology, saying he always regretted it whenever someone was offended by something he said. "But I am only human," he added, a weak excuse that wouldn't have passed muster around my kitchen table.

Sexism is something women in public life have to contend with, but I've never been willing to let it go unchallenged. Unfortunately, I had a little "friendly fire" of my own to contend with. Gail was rarely able to accompany me on the campaign trail because of work, but he was a regular presence on Facebook. To my dismay, he didn't hesitate to post raw musings there, including horribly inappropriate slams at women. For example, he directed this at Secretary of Homeland Security Janet Napolitano: "And am I suppose [*sic*] to give up my guns? As if! Traitorous skank!" Referring to the Benghazi raid, he called Hillary Clinton a "lying hag."

"What are you doing?" I demanded. I tried to explain to him—and shouldn't have had to—that he couldn't just go on Facebook and let loose because the mess would land in my lap. I'm not sure he got it, though. Maybe some part of him didn't mind publicly embarrassing me. I wasn't sure. But it was a distraction to be forced to apologize for my husband's vulgarities, especially when they were directed at women officials.

As we approached election day, I still felt like an underdog, but I was constantly heartened by the well wishes of Iowans. One of these was my sixth-grade teacher, Rick Gustafson—or as I knew him, *Mr.* Gustafson. He told a reporter that he still had a pillow my mom had embroidered for him with the names of all the students in his class. He spoke flatteringly about my intelligence and integrity, things I hadn't realized he'd noticed then, but his deeper message was about a strong work ethic, which was the way it was for Iowa farm kids.

I also had some impressive backup on the trail. Senator McCain arrived to ride the Squeal Mobile with me, and his presence energized the crowds and was a great honor for me and my staff.

People have asked me when I knew I was going to win. Of course, you never *know*, but in the last two weeks there were some signs. One day Kim Reynolds and I were campaigning together at a Caterpillar dealership in eastern Iowa, surrounded by heavy equipment. When we finished, one of my staff showed me some leaked results from a new *Des Moines Register* poll. It had me up by five points.

On election day, I voted in Red Oak, and then my family traveled to Des Moines for the results and an election night gathering of my supporters. I was tired to the bone. The past twenty-four hours had been a nonstop push through counties all over the state, and the first thing I wanted to do when we arrived at our hotel was take a nap.

That evening, we ate dinner in our room and watched the returns come in.

The media was saying that the voter turnout was higher than it had been in a midterm election for almost thirty years. The numbers trickled in during the evening, and by nine o'clock I was projected to win. The final tally gave me 52.2 percent of the vote to Braley's 43.7.

On my TV screen, I could see my supporters in a ballroom downstairs celebrating the win. I wanted to join them, but Braley hadn't yet called to concede. So, I waited. Finally, I got the call, and he was very gracious. I hugged my family and we headed downstairs.

Standing in front of my supporters, who were cheering wildly and waving signs, I was overwhelmed. "Well, Iowa, we did it! We did it!" and that set off a fresh wave of cheering.

I'd won other elections before this one, but it was particularly sweet because I'd started with so little. I flashed back to the days making calls in my attic back home, the querulous voices—"Who are you, again?" The long drives across the country roads to events that drew less than twenty people. The way their chanting voices— "Joni! Joni!"—would echo in near-empty halls. I'd come through it all, through more than a year of determination, and I'd won against all odds.

My attention was already turning to the work ahead. I would try to win the trust of Braley voters, to give every Iowan a reason to believe in me. I would begin right away to fulfill my campaign promises. But first, I wanted to offer an ode to the heartland that raised me.

Here in the fields of Iowa, our grandparents worked and dreamed of a better life for their children. Many, like mine, had very little to call their own, but they were determined to give their children a chance to succeed. And so they did. And because they did, they gave an ordinary Iowan extraordinary opportunities, opportunities that they could only dream of.

And in the Senate, that's the kind of America that I am going to fight for every single day. Every single day. An America where, no matter who your parents are or what neighborhood you grew up in, you have the chance to succeed. An America where it doesn't matter who you know. All that matters is how hard you work and what you can do. And working together—that's the America that we are going to build.

I grinned out at the people who had made it all possible. "It's a long way from Red Oak to Washington," I said. "Thanks to you, Iowa, we are headed to Washington, and we are going to make 'em squeal."

LEADERSHIP

My time in the state senate taught me that politics is tough everywhere, but nowhere is it as tough as Washington, D.C. Sometimes it's a swamp— that's a reality. But more often it's an insulated environment, stalled by bureaucratic entanglements, an absence of courage, and arcane rules. One of those rules was that freshman senators should be seen and not heard. I wasn't about to obey that one. For me, representing Iowa on Capitol Hill was all about leadership.

As a leader today, it's easy to forget where you come from. Political parties try to tell us how to speak, what to say, and what bills to support. The media frames everything in a certain light that's often unrecognizable from what we're trying to do. My goal as a leader is to cut out all that extra fat and spin. Above all else, I am a champion for Iowa; a defender of our armed forces; a voice for women; and an advocate for farmers and businesses. Leaders have to stand tall and listen to their consciences. When we forget that there are actual people behind those systems that we're leading, we're really in trouble.

Chapter Seven

FROM THE FARMLAND TO THE CAPITAL

Forget a leisurely transition period where I'd organize my wardrobe and make to-do lists for my new job in the United States Senate. Barely a week after the election, I was kissing Gail and Libby good-bye and heading to Epply Airfield in Omaha, the closest airport to Red Oak, to fly to Washington. A day later I was seated in a Senate conference room. It was orientation time—basically, back to school to learn the protocols and practices of being a senator. It was a little bit like being dropped in a foreign country without knowing the language or customs, and I flashed on a memory of my Ukraine exchange in college. As I sat there with my notebook open, I realized that although I was about to cram on how the Senate worked and its myriad rules, nobody was going to tell me *how* to be a senator. That was up to me.

On the campaign stump, I'd repeated my goals many times. I'd made promises I was determined to keep. But on a deeper level, I had to decide what kind of senator I wanted to be. I thought I knew. I wanted to be a senator who was true to myself. My friends had joked about my becoming "different" in Washington. "Don't let them change you," they instructed. I didn't plan to. I was determined to bring some "Iowa nice" to the capital, which meant I planned to be a collaborator, to work well with others to get things done.

I was joined for the three-day orientation by twelve other members of the "freshman class," all but one of them Republicans. In the election, Republicans had succeeded in winning back the Senate, with more than the six seats needed, and we'd now be in the majority.

My new colleagues were a mixed group, representing many parts of the nation and various levels of experience in government. Only two of us were women—me and Shelley Moore Capito, a seven-term congresswoman from West Virginia, who I hoped would teach me a few things about getting along in Congress. Other newcomers were Bill Cassidy, a gastroenterologist and congressman from Louisiana; Tom Cotton, a former Army captain and congressman from Arkansas; Steve Daines, a businessman and congressman from Montana; Cory Gardner, a congressman and former Senate staffer from Colorado; James Lankford, a Baptist minister and congressman from Oklahoma; David Perdue, a businessman from Georgia; Gary Peters, the sole Democrat, a congressman from Michigan; Mike Rounds, the former governor of South Dakota; Ben Sasse, a former college president; Dan Sullivan, a Marine Corps reservist and former Alaska attorney general; and Thom Tillis, former speaker of the North Carolina state house.

During orientation, we learned the complex and sometimes mystifying details of how to legislate, and the nuts and bolts of setting up our Senate offices. We learned about the typical range of constituent services—everything from flag requests (special flags that had flown over the Capitol were available), to expediting student nominations to service academies, to meeting requests and holding visiting hours. We were instructed in Senate culture, which had many customs and rules, and how to avoid ethics violations.

Stretching our legs, we toured our new domain, riding in the senators-only elevators to the underground that connects the three Senate office buildings—Russell, Hart, and Dirksen—to the Senate floor. A hundred-year-old train system chugs along at 15 miles per hour, but many of us prefer the walkways, where a brisk pace can keep our step-count up (15,000 to 17,000 steps on good days), while making it easier to outpace the ever-lingering press. On the other hand, our own little whistle stop could lend itself to collegial cama-raderie across party lines. Although much is made of how partisan Washington had become, I would find in the Capitol, as I had in the Iowa Senate, that for the most part senators try to get along on a human level outside the floor.

Walking into the Senate chamber for the first time, all of us were duly impressed. We'd seen it many times on C-SPAN, but being there was something else. The arrangement of the hundred seats reminded me of a movie theater, with a raised platform at the front and a visitors' gallery above.

The seating chart gets reshuffled at the beginning of every Con-gress, as senators come and go, but seniority plays a role. Technically, there's a Republican side and a Democratic side, but since there's rarely a fifty-fifty split, some senators end up sitting in the other party's territory. I was intrigued to learn that three seats are perma-nently assigned by Senate resolution: the desk once used by Daniel Webster goes to the senior senator from New Hampshire; the desk once used by Jefferson Davis goes to the senior senator from Missis-sippi; and the desk once used by Henry Clay goes to the senior sena-tor from Kentucky. Like any other seating chart, this one involves a lot of angling and horse trading, since obviously, certain seats are more desirable than others, and some senators like to sit together.

One seat was particularly coveted: the "candy desk," always stocked with a drawer full of sweets. This was a custom dating back to 1968, when George Murphy, a Republican senator from California, kept candy that he shared with his colleagues. When Murphy left after one term, the tradition continued. Since then the desk has been a favored assignment, held at various points by John McCain and Pennsylvania senator Rick Santorum. When I entered the Senate, Pennsylvania's Pat Toomey had just been seated at the candy desk, which delighted him, as Pennsylvania is home to the Hershey Company.

There's a moving-day feeling to the Senate office buildings after an election, with bulky desks and file cabinets and stacked boxes lining the corridors. I found my temporary office in the Hart Senate Building. It was the size of a storage room—I suspected it *had* been a storage room once—and was windowless. As we squeezed in during our first six months in Washington, it was another encounter with the power of seniority. Offices are delegated according to seniority, and I was number 98. But my staff and I got by. There weren't many of us yet. Later, I'd move to dark but spacious basement quarters in the Russell Building, before finally being assigned to a much sunnier office on the seventh floor of Hart in 2019.

Hiring a staff had been a top priority after the election. It was a challenge. I was going from the state senate where I had *no* staff to the U.S. Senate, where I had a full contingent in D.C. as well as five state offices. I was grateful for my military leadership experience, as I knew I would have to trust others to represent my office and constituents. I had less than three months to staff my D.C. office— chief of staff, legislative director, constituent services, press secretary, scheduler, and so on—and my state offices, which would be fully operational in Des Moines, Davenport, Cedar Rapids, Sioux City, and Council Bluffs. Since my predecessor was a Democrat, we had to do a complete staff overhaul, something that hadn't happened in decades.

My first hire was Lisa Goeas as chief of staff. Lisa had worked for Senator Tim Hutchinson for a decade, and she'd retired from Capitol Hill life after he lost his reelection bid in 2002. She was happily working for the National Federation of Independent Business when I called her. I told her straight out that I needed someone who knew the ropes and who shared my ideology. Thankfully, Lisa decided to accept. Together we sifted through applications for all of my offices.

At the end of the process I had hired a strong team. Most of my primary staffers were experienced in the ways of Washington, and I was grateful for that.

Another urgent matter while I was in town for orientation was finding a place to stay while in Washington. Gail, Libby, and I had talked about it and decided that since Libby was a high school junior, she'd stay in Red Oak with Gail until she finished school. They'd visit Washington when they could, and I'd see them back home on weekends. Many senators do it that way, not wanting to disrupt their families' routines. So Lisa and I looked for rentals, keeping budget considerations in mind. There's no stipend for housing, and D.C. is a very expensive place. Some members live out of suitcases in single rooms in basement rentals while others make it a practice to sleep in their offices. I could sympathize with the cost-saving advantages, but living at the office seemed like a terrible idea to me—not just physically, but mentally. I was lucky enough to find a reasonable place near the Capitol my first year. The following year Gail and I would get a small place about a mile from the Capitol, with room for the three of us. I was hoping it would encourage more visits while I was working in D.C.

One day during orientation, after a meeting with a group of new senators in Majority Leader Mitch McConnell's office, his chief of staff approached me. "Senator-Elect Ernst, the leader would like to speak with you. Can you stay for a moment?"

Feeling every bit the freshman being called to the principal's office, my first thought was, "Oh God, what have I done?" I was concerned. I couldn't imagine why McConnell wanted to speak to me.

I went into McConnell's office and he greeted me with a friendly smile. "We've chosen you to give the Republican response to President Obama's State of the Union," he said after we exchanged pleasantries.

I was briefly speechless. That's the last thing I'd expected! It was a huge honor, but to be honest it was intimidating, too. I'd expected to have a little time before I was in a position to address the nation! The SOTU response is a particularly challenging speech, with a history of being mocked. I decided my best course was to speak from the heart and be myself. But I was nervous.

I was sworn into office on January 5, 2015, in a simple but very moving ceremony, surrounded by family and friends, in the Senate chamber. Senator Grassley was there, as was my predecessor Tom Harkin, as well as General Tim Orr, my adjutant general in the Guard. As president of the Senate, Vice President Joe Biden officiated, calling each senator-elect and their family up in an assembly line–style process. When it was our turn, Biden held out a hand to Gail and greeted him, "Senator . . ." forcing me to say that *I* was the senator. This was followed by another embarrassing moment when Biden commented to Gail about how lovely Libby was and suggested he build a big fence around the house to keep the boys out. Gail laughed, but I was startled, and maybe my face showed it. It was such an inappropriate remark, and I felt momentarily sidelined as the guys chuckled. I imagine people would say that it was "Joe being Joe," but I didn't appreciate it or think it was funny.

I took my oath with my hand on the Bible that had belonged to my paternal grandmother, Pauline Culver: *I do solemnly swear (or affirm) that I will support and defend the Constitution of the United States against all enemies, foreign and domestic; that I will bear true faith and allegiance to the same; that I take this obligation freely, without any mental reservation or purpose of evasion; and that I will well and faithfully discharge the duties of the office on which I am about to enter: So help me God.*

Afterward, we had a reception in the Capitol Visitor Center, and Marco Rubio and Lindsey Graham, who had been very supportive during the campaign, came by. That evening, the Iowans who had traveled to D.C. for the ceremony held their own reception for me. As the day drew to a close, the solemnity of the occasion began to hit me.

I'd hardly had time to get settled when it was time for the State of the Union. I'd worked on my response over the holidays, and when the day came, on January 15, a whole ten days into my Senate career, I had a speech that I hoped would bring the heartland to the nation. I said in part:

> As a young girl, I plowed the fields of our family farm. I worked construction with my dad. To save for college, I worked the morning biscuit line at Hardees.... We know America faces big challenges. But history has shown there's nothing our nation, and our people, can't accomplish. Just look at my parents and grandparents. They had very little to call their own except the sweat on their brow and the dirt on their hands. But they worked, they sacrificed, and they dreamed big dreams for their children and grand-children. And because they did, an ordinary Iowan like me has had some truly extraordinary opportunities—because they showed me that you don't need to come from wealth or privilege to make a difference. You just need the freedom to dream big, and a whole lot of hard work.

Apart from anything else I said, this speech became known as the bread bag speech, because I told the story of wearing bread bags over my shoes as a child to protect them from the rain. The late night comics had a field day with the story, and many commentators went on the air to scoff at me and question whether it was really true. It seemed ludicrous to them. Of course, there was a flurry of memes—"Joni Ernst: Mother, Soldier, Bread Bag Icon"—and a Twitter handle, #BreadBags, featuring shoes shaped like bread bags. It gave us a laugh, but the story was true and it held a lesson: on the farm, we made do with what we had, and often we needed to be creative.

Plenty of folks told me about their own experiences growing up with only a single pair of good shoes and doing the same thing. I was touched to read a column by Peggy Noonan in the *Wall Street Journal*, recalling a similar experience. In her typical soaring prose, Noonan framed the bags as a glorification of the way real families live. She wrote: "America then had less in terms of things—shoes, coats, gloves. I can't say, 'And no one was ashamed.' At a certain point, it was embarrassing to for whatever reasons not have the right things, or to come across as haphazard or not taken care of. Kids want to fit in. But there were enough kids in difficult circumstances that you weren't alone."

Noonan's column hit the spot with me. A certain snobbery that afflicts our political world, encouraged by the media, does lead to mockery of those who come from rural America, and the cynical response to my story was typical. Noonan put things in perspective for those who grew up with rain boots, especially with her observation that the embarrassment of the have-nots was soothed by the reality that many of us were in the same boat.

When people asked, "How do you like Washington?" I'd reply, "I like it so much I come home every weekend." Whenever I landed back in Omaha and made the hour-long drive to Red Oak, I could feel my blood pressure going down with each mile. That was in spite of the fact that I worked just as hard on weekends in Iowa as I worked in D.C. At least in Iowa, I was in familiar territory. And although it might seem like a minor point, I didn't have to worry so much about how my hair looked—Senate women's hair was always a big topic of discussion in the nation's capital—or what I was wearing. Life in Iowa is more informal.

It's easy to think about election day as the ultimate moment of accountability for elected officials. But accountability is an ongoing process, and never more so than when I am in the state. I have to stay on my toes to keep up with local issues in Iowa so I can talk about them knowledgeably, whether at official events or in the supermarket parking lot. When I'm home, I have a sense of being needed and productive. In those early days, while I was feeling the pain of being away from my family, I was simultaneously experiencing a heightened sense of community.

One of the hardest things for me about Washington is living in the city, which is not particularly homey. I refer to D.C. as my FOB—a military acronym meaning forward operating base. My *home* is Red Oak. When I can, I use my evenings in Washington to work and downshift in my apartment, but many times I'm scheduled for gatherings with Iowans in town, or as the keynote speaker for an organization, or at a banquet. I try to accept as many of those requests as possible.

My committee schedule is always packed. From the start, I was very happy with my committee assignments. Although senators with seniority get first choice, they always ask us which committees we want to be on and try to accommodate us. I got pretty much everything I wanted—the Committee on Armed Services; the Committee on Agriculture, Nutrition and Forestry; the Homeland Security and Governmental Affairs Committee (which I would later replace with the Environment and Public Works Committee—a key committee of jurisdiction for my work on ethanol); and the Committee on Small Business and Entrepreneurship. (In 2019, I would add the Judiciary Committee, where I and Tennessee senator Marsha Blackburn became the first Republican women to serve.)

Votes are sprinkled all throughout the week. It just depends on what we have moving. But there are committee meetings or hearings pretty much every day we're in session. Sometimes we have multiple meetings at the same time, and we're all hopping in and out of our chairs and going back and forth. It keeps things lively.

Thank God—once again—for Senator Grassley. We probably agree on 98 percent of our votes, but on the rare occasion when we don't, we'll work with our staffs to make sure we don't throw each other under the bus. It's been a blessing having him there. He reminds everybody that he went thirty years having a good relationship with Tom Harkin, but their votes always canceled each other out.

Grassley is sharp as a razor and has a dry sense of humor—you have to be on your toes to keep up with him. He has a tendency, when he is talking about something that he's very adamant about, to raise his voice louder and louder as he speaks until he's at a point of almost shouting. At the end of the conversation, he'll always clarify, "I'm not mad at you," just in case you mistake his passion for anger.

When I first came to the Senate, there were a lot of long vote series. Grassley's desk is down in the front row, with a little chair next to it. He'd beckon me down to sit next to him, and we'd chat about life. People would often stop by to joke with Grassley, or tell him something important. Once a senator wandered over and looked at us enviously. "Man, I wish I could be the third senator from the state of Iowa," he said.

*   *   *

On a typical morning, I'm up at four thirty for a run on the Washington Mall.

The monuments are lit with a comforting glow, and every time I pass them, I have a great sense of tranquility—a feeling that no matter how chaotic our times, our nation holds. I know how much reverence all Americans have for these monuments and what they represent. I'm more of a jogger than a runner, and as I slowly pace myself past the World War II Memorial and down to the Lincoln Memorial, with the stalwart rendering of our great president, my mind travels back to those critical moments in our history. It's a valuable meditation for the start of days that can feel mired in trivial debates. The price of leadership is often disappointment, and on these jogs I think about how I can stretch myself to become larger than my challenges.

From my time in the military I've picked up the pleasure of being out in the open air. In the National Guard, we do ruck (foot) marches with heavy packs on our backs. I love ruck marches! Wanting to introduce my staff to the rigors and pleasures of a ruck march, on some mornings I've invited all of them to join me for predawn ruck marches around Washington. It's a volunteer-only exercise, at a brisk but not exactly military pace, and those who make the march always enjoy it. They appreciate the opportunity to see the city as it's waking up, talk informally about what's on their minds, and stretch their bodies and minds. It delights me to bring some of that military discipline to D.C., where it's ironically quite lacking.

I usually finish my morning run around 6:00. I head over to the Senate gym in the Russell Building to clean up, and I'm at my desk by 7:00. I've always been a morning person. I cherish the time I have alone before the phones start buzzing and the visitors line up outside my office. My staff has left me a stack of documents related to my committee meetings and the bills I'm working on, and I read and answer emails until the staff starts to arrive around 8:00.

Most mornings we have staff meetings, but on Wednesdays we start the day with a constituent coffee. Iowans who are in D.C. are welcome to come to my office, have coffee and a donut, and talk to me about whatever is on their minds. Usually, we take pictures, too. Sometimes Grassley will pop in, which is always a crowd pleaser. Many senators have these coffees, and I think most of us would agree that our favorite times are spent talking to people from back home. My staff and I look forward to our weekly coffees.

I also block out times to meet with constituents one-on-one in the afternoons. These meetings are serious business, not just meet-and-greets. If I'm called away for a vote, my staff will pitch in. We do everything we can to make sure Iowans are heard. This is the advocacy part of the job, when businesses, organizations, and individuals will state their cases about legislation they care about. Although there is a lot of reading in this job, the most effective way of learning is to hear firsthand about people's experiences.

I can't be the expert on everything, so I rely on my constituents to provide me with knowledgeable input on what is important to them. For example, in a recent farm bill I focused heavily on conservation while also ensuring we have farmlands available for beginning farmers. We have some wonderful conservation programs in Iowa, and we worry a lot about the quality of our soil and water. However, sometimes the programs have been used to block out farmers seeking farmland. Meeting with Iowans, farmer groups, and conservation experts gives me the input I need to craft legislation. I wound up getting my GROW Act put into law, which would help ensure that we keep the right balance.

Sometimes we win on issues that measurably change lives, and they happen to hit close to home for me. In 2008, I had been deployed with the National Guard during devastating floods in Cedar Rapids. When I came to the Senate there was a great deal of concern from visiting constituents that newer flood mitigation projects were ignoring past floods, such as the one in Cedar Rapids.

I was very interested in making this happen. I conducted meetings, held hearings, wrote letters, and engaged with people on the ground—the civics work director, the Army Corps of Engineers, and members of various agencies—trying to find a path forward. Through our tireless efforts, $117 million was finally approved in 2018, a decade after the flood, and best of all, it was retroactive. We could go back all the way to 2008 and apply those dollars. This was particularly important to me because I didn't think it was fair to grant money for recent flood events without taking care of communities that had been harmed in the past.

It's not unusual for these state-specific efforts to take years, because we have to convince our colleagues, including those who are not from rural areas, that our state needs are essential. It's all about staying the course and digging away. It's an example of how leadership is not always, or even often, flashy. It's intensive labor out of the spotlight. The retroactive flood assistance for Cedar Rapids didn't get headlines beyond the local press, but it's a big reason we do our jobs.

I'm always explaining to people why it takes so long to get some bills passed, and also why some bills never make it to the Senate floor for a vote. Most bills cannot get done unless they have bipartisan votes. This means we have to be very targeted and make sure legislation has broad support. The slow pace of Washington and its politics has been a source of frustration for me. For example, Minority Leader Chuck Schumer, like his predecessor Harry Reid, will often tell his caucus to not work with certain senators, especially if they're up for reelection on the other side. He doesn't want to hand them wins.

Even the actual vote process can seem confusing. People who watch the floor votes on C-SPAN often ask me what's going on there. They see senators during a vote wandering around the floor, coming in and out to record their votes, and for a viewer it's like watching paint dry. Although we're often voting on the most significant issues that affect the nation, there's usually little drama to the actual process.

When a vote is called, a system of bells and lights is activated in the Senate office buildings, so senators know they have fifteen minutes to come to the floor for a vote. (These days, we also get emails.) On the floor, the clerk begins calling names in alphabetical order. As each senator approaches the well of the Senate and announces his or her vote, the clerk reads it off. Of course, senators will drag in late, and that fifteen-minute vote may end up being a thirty-minute vote. It's not a game, so they try to do the courtesy of holding votes open until every senator that's available has been able to get there.

It's a very powerful statement that senators have to be physically present to vote, but it can be maddening if you're stuck on a plane or otherwise far from the Capitol. Some senators are especially purposeful about their voting record. Chuck Grassley hasn't missed a vote since 1993. Susan Collins also has a perfect voting record. I myself have rarely missed a vote, usually when visiting my daughter Libby at West Point.

At times votes will be scheduled well into the evening. There have been occasions of all-night sessions, or occasions when we've had to stick around until the middle of the night to vote, but that's rare.

There's a lot of behind-the-scenes wrangling that leads up to a vote—especially when the issue is controversial or when we're dealing with judicial nominees. Having five committees, there can be a lot of preparation for hearings. That includes sitting down face-to-face with judicial nominees in my office as part of the Judiciary Committee process. In some cases, I have concerns about a would-be judge's suitability, so these meetings allow me to share those concerns and see for myself how the nominee answers my questions. When a nominee is controversial, the home state senator acts as an advocate for the nomination, and talks to us individually about our support. This nod to the states is also a tradition of the Senate, and I think it's a good one. We are constantly reminded that we are not just there to serve an abstract national agenda, but to represent the people in our states.

It's a long-held norm that freshman senators should bide their time before introducing their first legislation, but these days new senators want to get out front on issues they care about as soon as possible. So, in the first months of being a senator, my staff and I talked about what would be my first legislation, and, of course, veterans issues were always at the top of my mind.

On February 15, 2015, Richard Miles, a forty-one-year-old Iraq War veteran and father from Des Moines, had visited a veterans' hospital, hoping to be checked in. Richard was suffering from PTSD, with intense bouts of anxiety and sleeplessness. Like many of the veterans I knew, Richard waited until his condition was critical before he sought help. But for some inexplicable reason, the hospital didn't admit him, and Richard went home. Later that night, Richard went out into the middle of the woods with no coat on and took all of the prescription sleeping pills he'd been given at the VA hospital. He lay down under a tree and froze to death overnight.

When I heard Richard's story I was heartbroken. Nobody should have to face that kind of despair alone. Why had the hospital turned him away? How had our system failed him? The VA could have done something, and they didn't. As I heard other stories similar to Richard's, I learned about the rapid increase in veteran suicides—one man I spoke to said he'd already tried to commit suicide twice. I found that the average wait time for a mental health consultation was thirty-six days—too long for men and women as desperate as Richard.

I decided to try to do something about it. On March 27, I gave my first floor speech, introducing the Prioritizing Veterans' Access to Mental Health Care Act, which would give more veterans quicker access to mental health services, until they were approved for comprehensive mental health care at the VA.

There was an immediate show of support for my bill. McConnell praised me, saying, "I expect it will enjoy broad bipartisan support, particularly with the sponsor having such firsthand knowledge of the needs of these returning veterans." Several senators signed on, including Grassley. The Wounded Warriors Project and Concerned Veterans of America offered their support.

I was elated. This was what legislating was all about—the chance to make a real difference in people's lives.

And then . . . nothing happened for a long time.

As a body, we introduce thousands of bills every year, and only a few hundred of them ever get through committee and have a real chance of passing. That's not to say that the ideas always die. Sometimes they get wrapped into other legislation, or pieced out in larger bills. Parts of my bill went into larger VA legislation that ultimately passed the Senate in 2018. This piecemeal approach is common these days in Congress. It's a way to get things done, and that's what matters.

Since I introduced that bill I've kept a single photo on my desk in my Senate office. It shows the honor guard presenting Richard Miles's daughter with the flag from his casket. Richard's boss gave me this picture because he knew how much Richard's story meant to me.

I never stopped working to provide help for veteran mental health services. In 2016, seeing that female veterans were committing suicide at six times the rate of nonmilitary females, I helped introduce the Female Veterans Suicide Prevention Act. This bill also received bipartisan support, and this time it reached the president's desk, and he signed it.

Our work is not only about passing legislation. For example, I'm very interested in what we can do to find resources for people to work themselves up out of poverty. On a trip through Iowa, I visited a program called Bridges Out of Poverty in Burlington, and it made a big impact on me. They take young men and women who have dropped out of high school and teach them skills, help them earn their GEDs, and then support them in getting into community colleges—whatever it takes to create a bridge to a better future. I spent an evening with these young people, who were preparing a chili and soup fund-raiser, and they were great kids who'd just needed a hand. Without our help they might become throwaways, pushed to the side. As someone who grew up in times of financial struggle, I felt very intensely that their plight could easily have been my own. So, in this and other situations I'll ask my state staffs to intervene and determine how we can be helpful to the program. And one thing I can always do as a senator is provide a letter of support as they seek assistance. In myriad ways, we do more than make laws. We advocate for the most vulnerable citizens and most worthy organizations so they have the tools to be successful.

Being a leader means being willing to assume risk. On the farm, my dad always told me that there would be risks, including droughts, shortages, and destruction. He taught me that in order to face these threats, we must assume the worst and prepare for it. I have taken this mentality with me throughout my career. I have assumed the risk of being a conservative political leader, enduring the backlash I receive for my opinions and policies. I don't mind principled debates with members of the other party. Sometimes an issue is close to my heart, such as making sure we provide resources for our fighting forces. I'll debate that issue every chance I get. I'm unwavering in my fundamental conservative principles of a strong national defense and a market-based economy. But I also believe that it's my responsibility to try to work with the other side and reach consensus when we can, so together we can serve our constituents' needs. I'm not interested in lobbing personal attacks at Democrats for the sake of proving that I'm a loyal Republican. For me, being a leader means rising above petty disputes and solving problems. This is the model Senator Grassley has set, and I guess it's an Iowa quality. It's also the right thing to do.

As my first year in the Senate drew to a close, I was faced with a sad decision—retiring from the National Guard and ending my twenty-three-year military career. During my Senate campaign, people had often asked me if I would retire from military service if I was elected, and I promised them that I would think about it seriously because I wanted to concentrate on the people of Iowa. Further, between traveling throughout Iowa and devoting time to my family, I didn't feel that I could balance all of it any longer. Legislatively, I wanted very much to use my platform to help the military and veterans, and I ultimately concluded I could better do that from the outside. I had loved my time in service, and it was hard for me to leave, but again, I made a commitment when I ran for the Senate to devote myself completely, and I knew that I would have to give up some things that were dear to me, and one of them was the Guard.

In November 2015, I attended my last drill for the Iowa National Guard. There was no big splash about it—just an ordinary drill, and I wanted to leave quietly and not make a big deal of it. But when I was done, as I was removing my gear, I felt the finality of the moment and got very emotional. The military role that had defined me for more than two decades was now over.

If there was comfort in closing this chapter, it came from the community that would very much remain a part of my life. In the years since I have spoken frequently with the soldiers and commanders I worked with, and have been able to give them a kind of support I could not when I was one of them. When they're in Washington to visit the National Guard bureau at the Pentagon, I'll make a point of moving my schedule around so I can invite them to visit me at the Capitol. Sitting there in my office I can hear them with a fresh perspective, and think about how I can bring a national spotlight to their issues. The way I see it, I didn't lose a military family when I left the Guard. I just found a new way to serve them.

I know that my service in the army as a woman has put me in a unique position among other senators, and I maximize this position as I work to instill new values and policies that will make America prosper. I won't be bulldozed by others and, instead, will stand up for the men and women who serve us. I understand the military on a deeper level than many of my colleagues. I speak out when leadership is required, even when that means bucking my party and the Trump administration. I opposed the administration's all-out ban on transgender people serving in the military because I felt that as long as you were able to serve and wanted to serve, you should be allowed to serve. I supported an amendment in 2019 opposing Trump's "precipitous withdrawal" of troops from Syria and Afghanistan. It is my duty to stand up for the men and women who remain a part of my community—and to do what is necessary to help them protect our freedoms.

Chapter Eight

WOMEN'S WORK

In Senator Barbara Mikulski's hideaway in the Capitol Building, china cups were set out for a Senate tradition—a "power coffee" for new women members, hosted by the woman known as the "dean" of Senate women. It was 2015, and this day's coffee would welcome two of us newbies, Shelley Moore Capito and me. All twenty women were gathered, chatting in a friendly manner. The mood was warm and supportive, despite the rugged election we'd come through—one to which we'd lost two female Democrats, Mary Landrieu and Kay Hagan.

I've been told that Senate women, under Mikulski's leadership, had once vowed not to campaign against each other, but that era had long passed by the time I came along. Elizabeth Warren had campaigned against me in Iowa, going so far as to call Braley "the real women's candidate." But at the coffee she welcomed me with sincere enthusiasm.

Now here we all were, colleagues, chatting politely and even joking. The power of Senate women, hard won over the years, was on full display under Mikulski's guidance. I would soon learn that this power club often transcended both party politics and male dominance. Mikulski, who joined the Senate in 1987, liked to talk about the indignities Senate women faced in her early years when she and Kansas Republican Nancy Kassebaum were the only women. There was no woman's bathroom off the Senate floor, so they had to use the same bathroom tourists used. In 1993, Mikulski led what she called a "pantsuit rebellion," where all the women showed up on the floor in pants—not allowed at the time. The rule soon changed.

The process of change could be slow, though. The Senate swimming pool was male-only until 2011! And long after other modernizations, including the installation of lactating rooms for new mothers, women senators had to endure the "little lady" syndrome, the gentlemanly putdowns that made it hard for them to have a voice.

Times have changed, but not entirely, so the women still look out for each other—and in the process, we collaborate on legislation and often overcome divisive partisanship. People have often said that women make good leaders because they are natural collaborators, and I think that is true. In general, women work without big displays of ego that get in the way. While we want to be recognized for our work, there's not an overwhelming need to get all the credit. We prefer to share the credit if it means getting things done.

I recalled my initiation into military leadership as the first female commander my soldiers would encounter. I vowed then to be strong without barking orders, and to listen to what the men and women in my command had to say. I was determined to bring a similar style of openness to the Senate—to be a leader who listened, and to reject a knee-jerk opposition to the other party. If that's a "woman's way," it is also an Iowa way.

Mikulski would retire in 2017, and her power coffees would cease, but one tradition she instituted is still strong. The women meet for dinner about once a quarter. These casual off-the-record gatherings are a welcome opportunity to share our stories and get to know each other. When Mikulski first set the tradition in motion, the dinners were held at the Monocle, a restaurant near the Senate that was a favorite watering hole of many elected officials. The women took special delight in having their dinners there, as it was kind of a men's club at the time. They'd enjoy the famous crab cakes in a room with framed portraits on the walls of towering male politicians such as Tip O'Neill, Barry Goldwater, John F. Kennedy, and Richard Nixon.

These days the dinners have become more varied in theme and destination, with the women taking turns hosting the events. Often, we look for interesting locales. For example, Amy Klobuchar hosted her dinner at the botanical center, and before we ate we took a tour of the indoor gardens, and learned about the different foliage—busy, high-level women taking time out to enjoy nature. It was a wonderful evening.

When my turn came, I decided to do something military themed because many of the women don't really engage with the military unless they're on the Armed Services Committee.

Rob Hood, assistant secretary of defense for legislative affairs, graciously offered to host us at the Pentagon. We were thrilled, of course.

On the big day, a shuttle bus came and collected the women. Shelley and I had an event, so we drove over separately with staff. When we walked into the secretary of defense's dining room, it was a wonderful scene. All the women senators were holding glasses of wine, and laughing and talking. Secretary of the Navy Richard Spencer was standing in the middle of a gaggle of senators, telling what appeared to be a very entertaining story. I could see that everyone was enjoying themselves. We visited a little bit, and then Spencer left and Hood took over.

Our tour guide was a young woman, a senior airman, who was knowledgeable and impressive. Some of the senators had never been to the Pentagon before, so it was a real eye-opener. After that we sat down to a beautiful meal of salad and baked chicken with vegetables and potatoes. Dessert was miniature pumpkin and pecan pies and apple pie à la mode—all served on the DOD's best china. What a treat for a small town girl from Iowa!

We went around the table and talked, as we always do, about what was going on in our lives. Because Thanksgiving was two weeks away, I ended the dinner by asking the women to share what they were thankful for. We talked about our families and our work, and several women mentioned being thankful for this unlikely women's support group we had. We were all thankful for the opportunity to be together, away from Capitol Hill, to share a glass of wine and a meal and decompress a little bit. To be human beings for an evening and share our friendship. I was proud to show the women a piece of my life as a veteran.

At these dinners, we focus on the women, and there's a code of silence about what we discuss. Generally speaking, the conversations are about how we're getting along in Washington, the challenge of raising kids while holding public office, and the ways we assert ourselves in our jobs—the normal kinds of talks women have when they go out together. We try not to be political at all. We don't talk about bills. We form relationships. And then we draw on those relationships when we are working on legislation.

As we work together, we also develop friendships. There are twenty-six women in the Senate now—five more than when I started. I have a fantastic relationship with my Republican colleagues—Lisa Murkowski, Susan Collins, Shelley Moore Capito, Marsha Blackburn, Martha McSally, Deb Fischer, Cindy Hyde Smith, and our newest senator, Kelly Loeffler. There are more Republican women than ever before. But my friendships also cross party lines. I have a close relationship with Kirsten Gillibrand, and I know her family. We've worked on bills together but also talk about our families and participate in a weekly Bible study group. Many times, I bond with my Democratic colleagues over shared passions reflected in joint legislation. That's not to say we always agree. We have fierce differences. But at the end of the day, we can be friends and we approach each other with the hope that our commonalities are greater than our differences.

I realize that out in the country there's an impression that we are hopelessly locked in a partisan standoff. But there is a great deal of bipartisanship, and I'll tell you why: *women*. Recently, I was at an event with a group of mostly moderate Republican women in Des Moines. The woman who hosted the event was a retired judge, and the attendees were all very well educated professionals, and they were interested in talking about bipartisanship. One after the other told me how tired they were of hearing about the divisiveness in our government.

I wanted to show them another side, so I started listing the bills I've worked on with Democrats, and at some point, I stopped and started to laugh because it became clear that most of them were women. So, when people ask me how we can combat partisanship in Congress, I guess the answer is to elect more women.

Being a woman in the Senate does require a conscious assertiveness, especially when you're on a committee that is viewed as a men's domain. I remember John McCain, when he was helping me campaign, insisted that I should be on the Armed Services Committee. That was great because it was an assignment I wanted. I knew I could bring my experience to the table.

Tom Cotton, Dan Sullivan, and I, all three veterans who came to office in 2015, were assigned to armed services because McCain pushed for us. But there were other men on the committee, older men, and I could feel their dismissive attitudes toward me.

I knew that when I spoke I had to have authority in my voice. I had to own my subject matter and leave no doubt in anyone's mind that I knew exactly what I was talking about. When it was my turn to question witnesses, I laid it out and let everyone know I didn't just talk the talk—I'd walked the walk, in combat boots.

I had street cred, and the senators who might have been inclined to dismiss me came around pretty quickly when they saw that I knew what I was talking about.

Sometimes I utilize a soft touch and find I can accomplish a lot by being a kind person who can work with people. But there are other times when a tough backbone is needed, even with members of my own party. During a White House meeting that included Iowa ethanol producers along with oil company representatives, Texas senator Ted Cruz and I were representing our different constituencies on the issue, on opposite sides of the table. Ted was dominating the conversation, and I grew frustrated that he wasn't letting the people we flew in from Iowa tell their stories. He just kept talking. Finally, I'd had enough. I slapped my hand on the table and said, "Ted, stop talking! The president brought these folks here to say their piece. You're not in the oil business or in ethanol, so you need to be quiet." He backed down after that and let our constituents have their say.

When young women in the military or just starting their careers ask me how they can handle male-dominated atmospheres where the men don't necessarily give them full respect, I tell them, "When you walk into a room, *own* that room. Make sure you know what your subject matter is, and show that you are the expert. Leave no doubt in any man's mind that you are equally capable, if not more capable, on any topic that you're passionate about." It's something I tell my daughter as well: when you show confidence, men will treat you with respect.

There's no question that women in the Senate take the lead when it comes to issues that impact women. In the spring of 2016, I joined with Missouri Democrat Claire McCaskill, my colleague on the Senate Armed Services Committee, to sponsor a bill tackling sexual assault in the military.

Before my election, Claire and Kirsten Gillibrand had engaged in a high-profile debate with competing bills on the issue. Kirsten was adamant that in order to ensure that assault victims were treated fairly, the chain of command should not be involved in assault cases. Claire disagreed, insisting that replacing commanders with civilian lawyers would undermine the command structure. Ultimately Kirsten's bill failed in the Senate and Claire's bill was passed. Now we were tackling the next step in the process: making it a crime under the Uniform Code of Military Justice to retaliate against people for allegations of sexual assault. The Military Retaliation Prevention Act was designed to strengthen the military response, increase transparency, require specific training for investigators, and ensure that each of the services adopt best practices to prevent and respond to instances of retaliation.

Claire and I made a strong team—she as a former prosecutor of sex crimes and me as a former military officer. Both of us had important personal backgrounds with these crimes. I relied on Claire for her knowledge of criminal justice, and she relied on me for my decades-long experience in the military.

I knew from my own observations that retaliation begins as a cultural issue. The culture of loyalty within the military ranks is strong, and that's a necessary part of doing the job. But culture can blind soldiers to the standard of integrity, and retaliation is always the wrong thing to do, even if you are trying to stand up for your fellow soldiers. A big part of our mission was forcing a reexamination of military culture and taking a firm stance on what is and is not acceptable. In no way, shape, or form is sexual harassment or sexual assault acceptable, and that goes for retaliation as well.

Among the most heartbreaking encounters I've had in Iowa are those that have been with military survivors of sexual assault, many of whom have never seen justice done. Far too often, these women end up leaving the service because they've been treated like outcasts. They tell me that when they reported the assaults they were told that they had to toughen up and let the abuse roll off their backs. It's a perverse definition of strength to expect victims to simply accept abuse and move on, especially when it means letting perpetrators go about their business without reprisal, only to abuse again.

The year after we introduced our retaliation bill, Claire and I collaborated again following a disturbing revelation about Marines United, a Facebook group of about thirty thousand active-duty and retired military who distributed hundreds of nude photos of female service members. Additional nude photo sharing sites were uncovered, and reports suggest the horrific activity was carried out by members in each service branch.

It was shocking, disgusting, and disheartening. Our bill, the PRIVATE Act, would try to halt such behaviors by making it a serious offense across all military services. An overwhelming number of senators voted in favor of the bill, which was folded into the annual defense bill.

Claire and I also worked together with a bipartisan group of colleagues, including Kirsten Gillibrand, Kelly Ayotte, and Shelley Capito, to address sexual assault on college campuses with the Campus Accountability and Safety Act, which was designed to strengthen protections for students and create transparency and accountability in institutions for how they handle reports. Piece by piece we were trying to chip away at the national crisis of sexual assault and harassment.

But the process of collaboration can get mired in partisan priorities and this is what happened in 2019 with the reauthorization of the Violence Against Women Act. When VAWA was first passed in 1994, its noble goal was to protect women in their homes, on the street, and anywhere they were threatened. In addition to defining a new set of offenses that could be prosecuted, the bill called for stronger penalties for sex offenses. It also established a support network, with grants for law enforcement, women's shelters, and prevention programs. The National Domestic Violence Hotline was established as part of this legislation. It was controversial at the time, and even women's groups did not back it wholeheartedly. But it eventually achieved bipartisan support and was signed into law.

In the coming years, the bill was up for reauthorization every five years or so, and each time there were fresh debates and also new advances. Not surprisingly, the political climate played a big role—but VAWA always got reauthorized. Now it was up for renewal once again, and I was happy to have Democratic senator Dianne Feinstein agree to work on a bill with me. But things didn't turn out the way I had hoped.

The history of the 2019 reauthorization effort speaks to the complexities of legislating. Remember, both houses of Congress have to approve a bill before it gets sent to the president to be signed into law. The VAWA reauthorization bill had originated in the House, which passed it and sent it on to the Senate. We then took it up and began redlining our own changes. In my estimation, the House bill contained a number of political talking points that made consensus more difficult. We spent more than six months working with different committees and stakeholders, trying to produce a bill that both

Republicans and Democrats could support. Meanwhile, I was told, Minority Leader Chuck Schumer was pressuring Dianne to just advance the House version of the bill with few—if any—changes. I couldn't resist thinking that Schumer had a problem with my being the lead author of the Senate bill and not wanting to produce a result with my name on it. Given the partisan mood that takes place in election seasons, I wasn't off base to think of that. At the same time, I knew for a fact that the House bill, loaded as it was with favorite Democratic conditions, would not get Republican votes.

The frustrating part was that Dianne and I mostly agreed on the central premises of the bill, and I thought it would be a terrible result if the whole thing got tabled because we couldn't agree on minor points. My basic position in such cases is to try, if we can, to remove nonessential portions of a bill when they threaten to drag down the larger package, and then to deal with them separately. We're not going to agree on everything all the time, but the American people deserve to have some action taken on these important matters.

Through long meetings between my staff and Dianne's staff we failed to reach a compromise. The biggest sticking point had to do with firearms. We agreed on keeping firearms out of the hands of those convicted of abuse, a protection that has bipartisan support. The problem is, the Democrats wanted to extend it too far by taking away guns from people retroactively and from those who were convicted of stalking, even if no violence had taken place. The lack of correlation between stalking and gun violence would make that provision very difficult for most Republicans to support.

I was interested in reality—what we could accomplish. As the saying goes, "Don't make the perfect the enemy of the good." In a blunt conversation, I told Dianne, "Republicans will see this as a gun grab. They'll say you're looking for ways to remove as many guns as possible, even if it's not justified."

I think Dianne wanted to agree with me, but she let me know that her hands were tied. In one of my final meetings with Dianne on the bill, she told me that she was going to introduce the House bill, essentially without changes, and I could introduce an alternative Republican bill. Then we'd see what happened. "The House bill will never pass in the Senate," I said. "It's a nonstarter." I couldn't personally support it, and I knew my Republican colleagues wouldn't, either.

This result was deeply discouraging. I believed that the product Dianne and I had been working on was solid. Even if we had stopped with everything that we agreed on, it would have been an improved bill. Why go forward with something that doesn't have bipartisan support?

I was especially angry with Schumer. I realized that we were in an election season. I understood all the optics arguments. In the campaign battleground, neither side wants the other to score big wins that they can take on the trail. But this was serious business that should have transcended politics. Our constituents expect us to work for them, not to polish our political ambitions. I respect Dianne, and I think she wanted to do a bipartisan bill, but Schumer put an end to it. What steamed me about it was that bipartisanship had always been one of my core values, but what good are my efforts if the other side won't budge?

Other Republican colleagues who are also committed to bipartisan bills have run up against the same Schumer treatment. I'll keep trying, hoping that Dianne and I can find a new way to get the bill going, but as we get deeper into the 2020 campaign season, what are the odds?

It's reached a point that we *always* seem to be in a campaign season or getting ready for one. We're crippled by the constant fight. I wonder, when *do* we stand up and be bold if we only have an eye on the next election? It was especially galling to me when a super PAC tied to Schumer issued several tweets claiming I was abandoning domestic violence victims. In his own public remarks, Schumer completely mischaracterized my views on domestic violence protections.

I was furious. "I do not need to be mansplained to by Chuck Schumer," I said. "I am a survivor."

In the end, I expect that we'll end up piecing together areas of agreement and making them part of a must-move bill. It would then go back to the House, where I hope strong bipartisan support and the necessity of moving quickly will see it through.

After the Democrats announced their bill, Dianne talked to me on the floor of the Senate. "I'd like to continue working on this with you," she said, and so we'll keep trying. We have to remember that the bills we pass have real consequences to people they affect—the women who live in threatening conditions. How do you tell them you couldn't reach a bipartisan agreement on measures that might save their lives?

While we were battling over VAWA, I was introducing another bill to help women who had been the victims of assault. The Compulsory Requirement to Eliminate Employees who are Perpetrators of Sexual Assault, or CREEP Act, was a simple, commonsense measure that would give government agencies the authority to fire employees or contractors who were convicted of or proven to have committed sexual assault. When I told a women's group about the bill, one woman said, "I can't believe we actually have to legislate that."

"Believe it," I replied.

The bill came about as we looked for additional areas of sexual assault that we could combat. We thought this was an easy, obvious one since we have some control over the federal government. So far, I've received tremendous positive response from Republicans, but I'm expecting serious blowback from the unions. It remains to be seen whether CREEP will make it to the finish line.

* * *

Being a woman in a legislative body where almost 75 percent of the members are men, there is always going to be a spotlight on you, a predictable sense that you are representing your gender. But I find that being a woman can be an advantage, as long as you are authentically yourself. Women tend to bring all of themselves to the table—you don't often see men running for office tagging themselves as "fathers," but my tagline is "Mother, Soldier, Senator . . ." putting mother first.

In public, I not only talk about my ideas and legislation, but also about growing up on a farm, raising my daughter, teaching Sunday school, and participating in my local community. I'm not much of a talking head, so you won't see me on TV unless I have something important to say. My constituents are more likely to see me in person. But I speak often on the floor of the Senate about my lived experience and the respect for Americans that I bring to my work.

I am conscious of being a leader, but when my Senate colleague Rob Portman first approached me in 2018 and suggested I run for an official Republican leadership position, my first response was that I'd have to think about it. Not that I couldn't do it. It's just that it was a big extra job, and I had to think about whether it was right for me. But as I gave it more thought, I realized that I really couldn't turn down the opportunity to project Iowa's voice and have a seat at the table when decisions are being made. So I said yes and announced my candidacy for vice chair of the Republican conference. Leadership positions are the result of a full election of party members, and I'd be running against Deb Fischer, my colleague from the next state over, Nebraska.

It was quite meaningful that both the candidates were women, since there hadn't been a Republican woman in leadership since 2010. There had been a lot of flack in 2017 when an all-male panel was assigned to work on the health care bill. The media had a field day with that, and some of my colleagues argued that gender shouldn't be a consideration. But in fact, women's voices need to be heard, especially pertaining to legislation that impacts their bodies, and that's why it's important to have women as influencers in the Senate.

Running for a leadership position meant campaigning, except it was among a very friendly voter base—my own colleagues. I began making appointments to meet with all the members of the conference, and some offered commitments. Others said, "No, I've known Deb for a long time. I'm supporting her." Still others told me, "I'm not going to say a word because both of you are my friends." One senator said, "Sorry, Deb asked me first. If you had asked first, I probably would have voted for you."

Whatever the outcome, I found the process of sitting down and talking about common goals with my fellow senators to be meaningful and often illuminating. I know Deb felt the same way. The job of vice chair of the conference is more than just being part of a larger leadership team. It's the position most involved in supporting the voices of the senators in a larger sphere.

The election was held on November 14, 2018, and when the votes were counted (by secret ballot), I was elected. It was a tremendous honor, but it was also a challenge. It was up to me to define the job as I saw it. There was no blueprint.

I began to organize weekly floor events, bringing members together to give speeches on the floor. The weekly speeches were organized around themes that were important for our party, and ended up being a wonderful opportunity for senators to talk about anything they care about, with the public tuning in on webcasts. For example, in the week leading up to Veterans Day in 2019, senators took the opportunity to offer heartfelt stories about our veterans.

Behind the scenes of those floor speeches, my staff helps senators organize materials and visuals. We also produce videos for our members to use on their websites. These are not campaign videos. Rather, their purpose is to profile a senator in a more personal way. Americans like to get to know their senators beyond a policy setting, and I help make that happen. Sometimes the videos are fun ways of connecting senators to their states.

In this way, with the eye and instinct of a woman, I like to think I'm helping to humanize members of the Senate as we've rarely done before.

Chapter Nine

SCRUBBING THE PORK BARRELS

I suppose that a lot of people thought my "Make 'em Squeal" campaign ad was just a clever way of getting public attention, and it surely did that. But I really meant it, too. So, in the early days of my term, I sat down with my staff and laid it out the way I saw it. "Iowans sent me to the Senate with the mission of cutting wasteful spending—and making Washington squeal," I told them. "Let's do it." I explained that it wasn't just an abstract issue. It mattered. The national debt was $18 trillion dollars in 2015, and that meant every Iowa taxpayer's share was growing right along with it. It's one thing when Washington is paying for critical needs, such as national security and infrastructure. It's another thing when money leaks out in waste or ridiculous expenditures that have no place in government. I told my staff that we'd target those areas of waste, and try to cut them through legislation. In my sights was also "pork barrel" spending— that is, government funds procured for unnecessary expenditures that help politicians get elected but serve no redeeming purpose.

There are those in Congress who never want to cut anything— who say, as they always had, "Shaving costs here and there is a meaningless exercise—small potatoes when you consider the size of the federal budget." But addressing waste is not just a matter of dollars and cents. It's also a matter of principle. It's a question of what we ask taxpayers, ordinary Americans who are struggling in their own lives, to foot the bill for.

Because the federal government is so big, there are plenty of areas of waste, so my staff was busy taking inventory of it. I charged them with finding out why the waste existed in the first place. Was it abuse? Was it fraud? Was it simply laziness in never examining it? Was it due to old, outdated laws that no longer applied? And having found the waste, what should we do about it? I couldn't just complain that the federal government was wasting our money. I had to find solutions, and try to get other members on board. And I believed strongly that those solutions had to be bipartisan—although, sadly, waste issues are among the least likely to get support from both sides of the aisle, for the simple reason that Democrats resist spending cuts. I was determined to try, however.

My efforts to cut waste haven't always been about wrangling with the biggest hogs. It was more like tangling with some obvious, seemingly small expenditures that people could get their heads around. It was a smart strategy to bring attention to the larger issue. In my view, when the government allowed frivolous expenditures, those inevitably snowballed into bigger expenditures, which were shrugged off as okay because no one was challenging them. We needed to draw the line somewhere—and then move on to the next line, and then the next. We were demanding that sanity be restored.

Government waste isn't a very sexy topic, but I've been pleased to receive wholehearted support from Iowans, who are extremely conscious of their tax bills, and who also have a strong moral code. For them, it's about doing the right thing, whether the savings are large or small.

One of my first "squeal" bills was a bit daring politically, as it challenged the cozy system of lavish perks for ex-presidents, which is the kind of elite giveaway that doesn't pass the smell test in places like Iowa.

When the Former Presidents Act became law back in 1958, during the Eisenhower administration, it made some sense. Before that time, there was no federal pension or system of financial support for former presidents. There were two of them alive at the time—Herbert Hoover and Harry Truman. Hoover was quite wealthy, but Truman was poor. Congress felt an obligation to former presidents to make sure they were taken care of—it was the least we could do for those who had served. Many people cited the story of Ulysses Grant, our eighteenth president, who was also a Civil War hero. After eight years in the White House, Grant had very little money. In his final year of life, suffering from throat cancer, he was so broke that he wrote a war memoir from his sickbed in order to leave his wife some income when he was gone. He died within days of completing the manuscript. Everyone could agree that a life of hardship was a sad end for a man who had served his country so valiantly. So, a law was passed ensuring that former presidents had a healthy pension, medical benefits, and some staff services. Later, Secret Service protection was added.

But let's face it: today being a former president is a pretty sweet gig. Former presidents rake in millions of dollars from speaking engagements, consultancies, and other endeavors, while taxpayers are on the hook for their travel costs, office staff, computers, phone bills, postage, and other ordinary expenses. Our Presidential Allowance Modernization Act, dubbed the Presidential Perks Act, was designed to bring some discipline and fairness to the system, with a formula for payments. For every dollar an ex-president earned above a certain (very generous) amount, we'd take a dollar away.

The Presidential Allowance Modernization Act was introduced

in the House of Representatives by bipartisan cosponsors, Jason Chaffetz of Utah and Elijah Cummings of Maryland, and was passed on January 11, 2016. My companion Senate bill, cosponsored by Mark Kirk of Illinois and Marco Rubio of Florida, passed the Senate on June 21.

And then President Barack Obama vetoed the bill, claiming it "would impose onerous and unreasonable burdens on the offices of former presidents."

The White House noted that Obama had consulted with the four other surviving presidents—Jimmy Carter, George H. W. Bush, Bill Clinton, and George W. Bush—and implied this was a consensus view. But were the concerns warranted?

The White House noted two areas in particular: staffing and security. They said that if the bill became law, it would "immediately terminate salaries and all benefits to staffers carrying out the official duties of former presidents—leaving no time or mechanism for them to transition to another payroll." But this gloom-and-doom scenario was hardly the case. The bill stipulated only that *wealthy* ex-presidents would have to foot some of those expenses themselves, which seemed fair if they earned a level of income unthinkable to most Americans.

In addition, said the White House, the bill would have made it harder for the Secret Service to protect former presidents. But that was absolutely untrue. Lifetime Secret Service protection was established for former presidents, their spouses, and children under sixteen in a separate act in 1965. A 1994 statute limited that protection to ten years for presidents inaugurated after 1997, but lifetime protection had been restored under President Obama in 2012. Secret Service protection was not impacted by our bill.

So, our bill was not popular among former presidents, although

I would have thought the spirit of fair play alone would have convinced them. I was disappointed that Obama didn't see the law as the right thing to do—choosing instead to unfairly feather the nests of those in an exclusive club that he would soon join. I was further disappointed that he did not heed the clearly bipartisan support in Congress.

After the House decided not to try to override Obama's veto, we went back to work to modify the bill, and we reintroduced it in 2019 with bipartisan support. My Democratic colleague Maggie Hassan from New Hampshire was the lead on the Democratic side. As Maggie put it, "It's common sense." New Hampshirites don't like to pay for pork any more than Iowans do. And there's something unseemly about very wealthy men feeding at the public trough. Since leaving the presidency, the Obamas have scored a $65 million book contract, and more recently, a Netflix deal that will earn them untold millions. Do they really need our money?

During my first term, I've sponsored numerous bills that attack pork in federal spending. But some are more outrageous than others. Probably the example that gets the most squeals is a little-known system of "swag" expenses that costs taxpayers $1.4 billion a year. We all know what swag is—those free giveaways that companies use to promote their products. Who would have thought the government needed to promote itself so expensively? It's an advertising machine, packed with drink koozies, pens, key chains, snuggies, fidget spinners, stress balls, coloring books, tote bags, and more.

The first question that comes to mind is, why do we need to advertise federal agencies? Sure, there are meaningful government programs where promotion is legitimate. A magnet reminding a pregnant woman to take her prenatal vitamins might be a legitimate activity of an HHS program. But I question whether a government agency should purchase items just to advertise that it exists. So, in 2019, I introduced the Stop Wasteful Advertising by the Government Act—or SWAG—Act.

Investigating this abuse was a real eye-opener. Here we are, battling escalating budget deficits and calling on Americans to tighten their belts, but we're spending $1.4 billion a year on swag.

For me, the most ridiculous example of swag waste has to be the custom-made costumes for mascots. At a cost of $250,000 a year, it doesn't exactly break the budget. But it does offend the conscience.

Various federal agencies have decided that they need mascots to get their message across to the American public:

The Department of Agriculture has "Sammy Soil" and "Ruby Raindrop," agency mascots that allegedly promote conservation.

The Department of Energy has the off-putting "Green Reaper," a play on the Grim Reaper that holds a flower instead of a scythe.

The Department of Defense has "Bite the Lightbulb," whose purpose is murky—to promote the U.S. Navy Installation Command's Shore Energy Program.

"Franklin the Fair Housing Fox" is HUD's mascot, designed to promote "greater housing opportunities for all." I can think of many ways to promote fair housing, and a mascot fox isn't one of them.

"Rex the Ready Lion" comes from the Department of Homeland Security's Emergency Management Agency, to help people prepare for natural disasters.

NASA spent more than $30,000 on a Martian costume party in Mars, Pennsylvania, as a promotion.

The propaganda is not limited to freebies and cartoon characters. The State Department, for example, spent $630,000 to buy fake Facebook fans and paid to send social media influencers on a two-week junket from abroad to the location of popular U.S. television shows to promote American values. This is just stupidity.

The SWAG Act would nip this type of excess in the bud, by prohibiting the federal government from spending money to create mascots to promote an agency, program, or agenda, unless such a character is explicitly authorized by statute—like "Smokey Bear" or "Woodsy Owl." It would also prohibit public relations and advertising for purely propaganda purposes, allowing exceptions for military recruitment and other specific functions that are authorized by statute. It would prevent the purchase and distribution of "swag"—merchandise such as buttons, coloring books, fidget spinners, key chains, koozies, or stickers, for example—by federal agencies, unless explicitly authorized by statute, like medals awarded for sacrifice or meritorious service. To hold agencies accountable, there would be public disclosure of public relations and advertising expenditures.

There was a minor dustup when I first introduced the bill. Senator Martin Heinrich from New Mexico approached me on the Senate floor, very agitated. "*Really?*" he cried. "You're trying to get rid of Smokey Bear?" Smokey is from New Mexico, based on a real bear that was rescued from a fire.

I said, "No, Martin. Smokey Bear is exempt."

He wasn't convinced, and went on about Smokey for a while. "You need to read the bill," I said finally. I wasn't making it up. Smokey Bear is a national treasure. However, most of the mascots were expendable. If we're serious about disaster preparedness, for example, let's enhance the local agencies responsible for citizen alerts and information, not put a cartoon fox on the air.

I encountered the same outcry over Woodsy Owl, the famous Forest Service mascot whose motto is "Give a hoot—don't pollute." Also exempted. But all the others would get the boot. I don't think taxpayers want to shell out for the "Green Reaper"!

Needless to say, the SWAG bill got plenty of attention. As usual, there was the defense: "$1.4 billion, that's not a lot of money." This argument is offensive, but the number crunchers tried to make it stick. One guy figured out that the cost divided by the entire U.S. population would only come to .0002 cents per person. "What's the problem?" he asked. The problem is that it all adds up.

The $1.4 billion we spend on advertising gimmicks is twice the amount the federal government dedicates to breast cancer research. What matters more—that I get a free stress ball at an agency event, or that I actually know my dollars are going for something worthy? If you directed that $1.4 billion to breast cancer research, or food programs for the poor, or veterans services, it would be a big deal. Instead we throw money away on tchotchkes.

Another area of waste that people find disturbing is the cozy system of insider payoffs for government work. If you hired a contractor to build your house, and he was behind schedule, and in addition to that, he screwed up your plumbing, what would you do? If you were the federal government, you'd pay him a bonus!

Behind the scenes, federal agencies are paying millions in bonuses to contractors, even when the projects go nowhere. How is this possible? In the federal system, bonuses are commonly used as incentives for productivity, but the scandal is that often these bonuses get paid even when the work is below standard or doesn't get completed. Federal regulations technically prohibit bonuses for substandard work, but they're paid anyway.

Here are two shocking examples: The Department of Defense inspector general reported that the Pentagon had been paying out hundreds of millions of dollars in unearned bonuses to contractors, including $10.6 million to a contractor who failed to provide the necessary parts purchased for fighter jets, which created "a life and safety concern" for airmen. In another instance, NASA's inspector general revealed that the space agency has been paying massive bonuses totaling more than $500 million to the contractors of the next manned moon mission, which is likely to be billions of dollars over budget and years behind schedule as a result of those contractors'"poor performance."

What's the deal? Even with prohibitions to unearned bonuses, they still get paid, and we're not talking about small change. When I saw the evidence, I was angry, and I wanted to expose the agencies and put an end to the practice. My Bogus Bonus Ban Act requires government contracts using award fees to link the awarding of bonuses to outcomes, defined in terms of program cost, schedule, and performance. It directs every federal agency to set standards for determining which agency officials are authorized to approve the use of awards and incentives, while also establishing firm guidelines for judging contractor performance—something that should have been done all along. It would also hold agencies accountable by forcing them to make data available on any bonuses paid, and return to the U.S. Treasury any funds set aside for bonuses that are not paid due to the contractor's inability to meet the established criteria.

Fiscal responsibility is something we all teach our children, so we should practice it ourselves. Just as egregious as the undeserved bonuses is the way large projects are allowed to go on and on without accountability about getting finished.

For example, a high-speed train that was supposed to connect San Francisco and Los Angeles was thirteen years behind schedule and $44 billion over its original price tag. According to the California state auditor, the project was plagued by "flawed decision making" and "poor contract management."

My 2019 Billion Dollar Boondoggle Act addresses that. Basically, it states that if you have a project that is a billion dollars over its original cost estimate (yes, that's billion with a *b*), or it's so long beyond the time it was supposed to be completed, then we have requirements that have to be met, or that project will be canceled.

It's common sense that if you have a project that's just hanging out there costing money without getting completed, that project needs some serious oversight.

It's frustrating that when there *are* cost saving measures they're often misguided. For example, in 2018, the Department of Defense tried to shave costs on its electronic equipment by buying $30 million worth of equipment manufactured by Chinese companies with known cybersecurity vulnerabilities, despite repeated warnings by other government agencies. Spending millions in taxpayer money on computers, printers, and other tech equipment knowing it could compromise our security makes absolutely no sense.

The most damning report came from the DOD's own Joint Chiefs of Staff Intelligence Directorate, which cautioned that computers and handheld devices produced by Lenovo, the largest computer company in China, could introduce compromised hardware into the DOD supply chain. They also pointed out that years earlier, in 2006, the State Department had banned the use of Lenovo's computers after finding them used for cyberespionage. In 2015, the Department of Homeland Security once again warned about preinstalled spyware in Lenovo's computers. Yet the Department of Defense has gone ahead with more than $2.1 million in Lenovo products, even as its own inspector general warned about that and thousands of other technologies, to the tune of $32 million, that were vulnerable to hacking.

This raises all kinds of alarm bells, as I pointed out in a very tough letter to Deputy Secretary of Defense David Norquist. A letter hardly seems enough, I know. But many in Congress are truly concerned about this issue, and we're looking for ways to assert some legislative muscle. What good does it do to cut costs if we give away our security in the process? We live in a time when war can be waged through technology, so we can't just hide our heads and ignore the risk.

Each month I publish a "Squeal Award" on my website, which cites the agency or program that is most wasteful, corrupt, or unresponsive to fiscal standards. There are always plenty of candidates. Some people find the awards entertaining, but there is nothing funny about wasting taxpayer money. Today we are more than $22 trillion in debt, which is more than $67,000 for every Iowan.

When I'm sitting with locals at the Rainbow Café in Red Oak, which is like eating at a big family dinner table, a favorite topic of discussion is how dissociated Washington is from the rest of the country. My neighbors really do see Washington as a swamp. The swamp thrives inside a clogged bubble of Washington, D.C. The more I see in Washington, the more bothered I've become by the bubble. So, I finally asked, why do all of our federal agencies have to be centered here? Why not distribute them more broadly throughout the country—closer to the people who are actually affected by their decisions? In particular, I began to imagine agencies like the Department of Agriculture, the Department of the Interior, and the Environmental Protection Agency being located closer to their primary stakeholders—the folks who know the needs of their states, farms, and businesses best. And in the process, we would see more job creation and greater opportunities for communities across the country.

The federal government employs more than two million civilians. According to *Governing* magazine's online database, about 20 percent of those civilians are based in Washington, D.C., Virginia, or Maryland, even though those areas only make up about 5 percent of the U.S. population. Currently, the headquarters of nearly all executive branch agencies are clustered in and around Washington, D.C., concentrating hundreds of thousands of jobs in the region.

In Iowa, we often feel that the attitude of these agencies is kind of "out of sight, out of mind." What if they were in the midst of us? Not only would they be more responsive, but the move would also bring good, stable jobs to the heartland.

But there is a reason all government agencies are located in Washington, D.C., in the first place: The federal law that required it was passed in 1947, and I suppose it made some sense in an era when communications were limited and coordination with people not in the same city was difficult. But we live in an entirely different environment now, where most communications don't happen face-to-face but rather electronically. The rest of America has caught on, with videoconferencing, digital files, and text messaging. The federal government remains stuck in the 1940s.

It makes sense for agency operations to be distributed throughout the country. The Trump administration recognized this and relocated two Agriculture Department agencies to Kansas City, along with an Interior Department agency to Colorado. That was a step in the right direction, and I'm hopeful that Congress will follow suit, which is why I introduced the Strategic Withdrawal of Agencies for Meaningful Placement—or SWAMP—Act in March 2018.

The SWAMP Act would repeal the section of the U.S. Code that requires federal agencies and departments to be located in Washington, D.C. It would then prohibit agencies currently headquartered in D.C. from entering into new lease agreements, making significant renovations to their existing locations, or beginning construction on new facilities in the area, while establishing a competitive bidding process to allow states and municipalities to compete for the relocated headquarters. The act exempts the Executive Office of the President, the Department of Defense, and all other national-security-related agencies that must be in close proximity to Congress and the White House.

It's been an uphill battle getting the SWAMP Act to the finish line because it's an institutional change, and Washington recoils from anything complex and potentially messy in the short term. There was an immediate hair-on-fire reaction to my bill because it would require such a physical upheaval. The agencies that would ultimately benefit were even defensive, citing the great work they're already doing from afar. But just because we've long done things one way doesn't mean we can't shift gears to make our taxpayer-funded operations more effective. There's nothing inherently sacred about the capital. I'm still fighting to get this bill passed.

Those of us from the often-overlooked heartland have repeatedly found ourselves on the outs when Washington-based agencies issue directives that ignore our reality. A good example is the 2015 Waters of the U.S. rule issued by President Obama's Environmental Protection Agency and the Army Corps of Engineers, which established which waterways, large and small, would be under their purview.

It was nothing more than a power grab, allowing the federal government to regulate 97 percent of the land in Iowa. There was an uproar among officials representing our state, as well as representatives of other heartland states. The rule was a threat to farmers, manufacturers, and local businesses. We felt that the agency simply failed to understand our needs or what constituted productive action. That rule was repealed under the Trump EPA, but it's not enough. Since federal agencies have oversight over the most critical issues affecting us, they need to be close to the heart of our communities, to witness firsthand the effects their rules have.

These types of rules—made by Washington-based bureaucrats—are often nonsensical or, in this case, have harmful impacts on the populations affected. Had the folks writing this rule been in an office in the Midwest, they might have taken a different approach, know-ing how this rule would impact communities outside of D.C.

We don't have to be stuck in the swamp. We have the power of our imaginations and our drive for growth and betterment. We can decide as a nation—by encouraging our elected officials—to level the playing field by making our government agencies not servants to the elite, but true partners in our development.

GRIT

On the farm, we don't have the option of throwing in the towel. If we didn't plant and harvest, there would be no crops, and if there were no crops, there would be no sustenance. Farmers don't have the luxury of sleeping in—it's a daily grind: up at dawn, out in the fields. As kids, we didn't have the choice of not doing our chores. They were essential to the life of the farm. So that grit, that determination to never give up, was bred in me. If you talk to most Iowans, you'll find the same spirit.

Grit is not synonymous with success, although successful people often have grit. The surprising factor is their ability to get back up in the face of failure. We all fail sometimes, but the question is "What next?" It takes courage to acknowledge your flaws and still stand tall and try again. In my life in Iowa, I've met many people who have lost everything, yet found a way to come back. In the military, I've known men and women who have been horribly injured, but who have shown the courage to lead incredible lives.

Grit may be a quality of rural life, but I've discovered that it's most important during times of crisis—wherever you happen to be—when your foundations get pulled out from under you.

Chapter Ten

A PRIVATE BATTLE

I met with presidential candidate Donald Trump in July 2016 at his golf course in Bedminster, New Jersey. He was in the process of choosing a running mate, and I was there for an interview. After only a year and a half in the Senate, I was flattered to be having this meeting, and glad that Trump was thinking about a woman for the job.

We had a lengthy and productive conversation that included lunch on the patio of his golf club. It was immediately apparent to me that Donald Trump wanted to help people in our country who had been promised help, but were left behind by other politicians and their rhetoric for decades. He asked me a lot of questions, particularly about my time in the military, and was a very good listener. At around the halfway point in our meeting, his wife, Melania, joined us. She was so lovely to visit with, very intelligent and clearly very engaged in the campaign. I so appreciated her taking the time to sit with us for the remainder of the meeting. It was truly a highlight.

As exciting as the experience was, I told Trump that I would have to pass on being considered. I felt strongly that Iowa had to be my focus, and that's where my heart was. It also wasn't the right thing for my family at that point.

Libby was a high school senior and my husband was on the

verge of his second retirement, so I was looking forward to some big changes in our household, as Libby went off to college and Gail—I hoped—would be able to better balance his time between Iowa and D.C., while I was there during the workweek. I had visions of him volunteering at Walter Reed Medical Center or engaging with veteran groups and causes. I told him quite seriously about the Senate spouse activities, and he replied—also quite seriously—that he wasn't about to hang out with a bunch of women.

Trump chose Mike Pence as his running mate, which was an exceptional choice, and I spent the next year busy in the Senate and preparing Libby to graduate and leave for college. To Gail's and my tremendous pride, Libby was accepted to the U.S. Military Academy at West Point. Our smart, purposeful girl had decided to follow her parents' footsteps and go into the Army. No matter what career she eventually chose, I was heartened that she had learned from me not to be intimidated about entering a challenging, male-dominated arena. When she entered, only 20 percent of West Point cadets were women, about the same odds I faced when I joined the Senate. I had plenty of advice to impart about being strong and confident in a military environment, but Libby also had qualities I didn't necessarily have when I started out, including maturity and common sense beyond her years. She also had the experience of having a mother who served in the National Guard, so she knew some of what to expect.

Like every parent, I was sad to see my daughter leave the nest, but there was an extra advantage in her attending West Point, in that she would be geographically closer to me. My favorite excursions would become the precious occasions when I could drive up to New York for the few weekends when parents were allowed to visit.

Once Libby was gone and he'd retired, Gail would only rarely come to D.C. In fact, he seemed to grow more resentful of my position. In the early days of my being a senator, it had been a novelty to him, and he'd enjoyed the attention it brought him from friends. But when the novelty wore off, he wasn't as interested anymore. As for volunteer work, that held no interest for him. "I'm retired. I've paid my dues," he told me when I suggested various activities. It soon became clear that he had no intention of joining me. (Unknown to me, Gail had told both Libby and my mother the previous year that if I were to become vice president, he would not live with me at the residence in the U.S. Naval Observatory.)

People tend to pay an inordinate amount of attention to women legislators' personal lives—far more than men, who are allowed a privacy zone around their families. So I often got the question "Where is your husband?" My assertions that he was busy back home in Iowa became increasingly hollow. I couldn't imagine what he was doing with his time, but I felt wounded that he didn't want to spend it with me.

I didn't have the luxury of stopping everything to focus on my marriage. I had the biggest job of my life, full of obligations and the daily need to be on my game. But as the years passed, it was increasingly clear that Gail had never bought into my new reality. He thought I was living some kind of high life in Washington, full of fancy dinner parties, when for the most part a night out for me meant pizza at the Union Station Pizzeria Uno or a bowl of cereal or a salad at home. When I had meals with my colleagues or constituents, Gail characterized them as me "going out with other men." I was in the ridiculous and ultimately hopeless position of repeatedly explaining my job to a husband who thought I was stepping out on him.

Our nightly phone calls were becoming increasingly tense. Before hanging up, I always said, "I love you," and the most he would say was, "Well, good night." It wasn't much better when I was home in Iowa. I had a job to do there, too, traveling the state, and Gail was impatient with my absences. But when I stayed home and suggested

we do things together, he usually brushed me off. He was also acting strange. He spent a lot of time on Facebook, but when I'd walk
into the room he'd quickly put his phone down. I noticed that he
set a screen lock on his phone, something he'd never done before. I
was confused about what he wanted, even as he drew further away
from me.

Did it occur to me that there was another woman? I suppose
there were fleeting thoughts, especially given our earlier experience,
but I didn't consider it seriously. It had been a decade since the crisis
that nearly ended our marriage, and Gail had been very supportive of
me through my state senate terms and my run for the U.S. Senate. I
figured his moods and strange behavior were due to the uncertainty
around retirement and the effort to find a way to define himself. Gail
was a proud man who needed people to look up to him. But whatever he was going through, it was having an impact on me. I started
to dread being home. I hated the way Gail made me feel, with his
constant complaints and guilt trips. But I kept my fears to myself,
convinced that we were just going through a rough time. I didn't
even tell my mother.

One weekend when I was home, Gail told me he wanted us to go
down to Fort Leonard Wood and have lunch with a friend's son who
was getting ready to deploy as a contractor in Afghanistan. It was a
five-hour drive, but I thought it would be good for us to spend that
time together, so I agreed. We got down there and had a really nice
lunch with the young man, and headed back home by midafternoon.

About an hour into our drive, Gail suddenly said, "I want a
divorce. I don't love you like a husband should." He spoke without
emotion, staring ahead through the driver's window.

I was blindsided, stunned. I didn't know what to say. I felt tears
instantly filling my eyes. I was completely unprepared for his declaration, speechless in the face of his cold resolve. He continued to

drive, his face a stone mask. At that moment, with at least four hours left in the drive, I was afraid to say anything. It was an agonizing, silent ride.

By the following day, I had more of a grip on myself. I was convinced that Gail didn't really want a divorce—his words were a cry for help. I told myself we were going to work things out. We'd been married for twenty-six years. We'd get through this.

But when Gail dropped me off at the airport for my return to Washington, he looked grim. Late that night, he sent me a text that read "Don't call me this week . . . I need to do some soul-searching and praying, and I can't talk to you." I was insulted that he'd decided to make the rules, but it did me no good to argue. It was one of the most humiliating situations of my life.

I went to my office the next day, determined to focus on my work. But at odd moments, I thought of Gail, and the whole thing made no sense to me. What would cause him to just decide, without any discussion, that our marriage was over? When I looked at Gail's emails, I understood what was going on. It was all there—clear evidence of an affair with a woman who I discovered had been his high school girlfriend. They were writing about how he needed to see a lawyer, and fantasizing about how they'd have a wonderful family life with Libby. They were making plans to live together. The emails predated Gail's request for a divorce by about a year. They even fantasized over email about the eventual graduation party that they would throw for Libby at the end of her time at West Point, as if I didn't even exist. They went on to share plans for the house they were going to have in Arkansas or Florida after I was out of the picture, and to discuss budgets for their life together, right down to the allowance for her dog's food every month and her hair upkeep. It seemed as if they had it all planned out.

It hurt to read Gail complain that I had never been around while

Libby was growing up. This simply was not true. Apart from my year in Kuwait—not unusual in a military family—I was rarely away from Red Oak, except for required drills. Even when I was in the state senate, I was only gone three nights a week for the first four months of the year.

The rest of the time I was home. Conveniently, he didn't mention all the times he'd been away.

In addition to how hurt I was by the unfair charge that I was an absentee parent, it also went to the heart of what it means to be a woman and a mother in our times. This wasn't the 1950s! My life was not that much different than that of any woman pursuing a career and figuring out ways to combine work and family. Libby and I are very close, and I always felt proud of being a role model for how much a woman could achieve, while still being a loving, engaged parent.

As I printed the emails, I called Lisa, my chief of staff, to come in. She knew something was wrong and I wanted to let her know what was going on. I pointed wordlessly to the stack, and she started to read. Her eyes widened and her face flushed. "Don't read these, Joni," she instructed, holding the pages away from me, concern in her eyes.

"I already have," I told her, crying. I felt sick. And I didn't want to let Gail know that I knew.

Several weekends later I drove up to West Point to do a ruck march with Libby. I threw myself into the event, hoping Libby wouldn't notice anything amiss with me. Thankfully, she was happy and thriving, and I pulled off the deception. The next weekend, Gail and I would be returning to West Point together for Libby's Acceptance Day. Acceptance Day is a ceremony and parade welcoming the plebe class into the Corps of Cadets, and it's a big deal.

Gail flew into Washington the night before, and we drove up

together. On the way, he said, "We have to tell Libby about the divorce this weekend." I felt sick about the idea, but Gail was insistent.

When we arrived that afternoon, Libby was occupied for the next few hours, so we sat together on the front porch of the Beat Navy House. I couldn't keep it in any longer. I asked him, "Who is this woman to you?"

"What woman?"

"Gail, I read your emails."

To my amazement, he broke down and started crying. "She is the one I should have been with all along," he blubbered. "I never should have married you. She was always meant to be my wife." As I stared at him with my mouth hanging open, he went on about how he'd loved her since high school, and after his first divorce, he'd looked for her, but by then she was already married. He'd been pining for her all this time. After he retired, he'd looked for her again, and she'd been married, but she was willing to leave her husband for him. Now, he said, "I want to do the things I want to do, and I can't do them with you as my wife." I was crushed by his words. It was one thing to say that we'd grown apart. But Gail was cutting me deeper, saying after twenty-six years that we never should have been married in the first place. That hurt more than anything.

The weekend was very busy, and we spent a lot of time with Libby and her fellow cadets. There was never a chance to talk to her alone. We took her and her friends out to eat, and I remember sitting in the restaurant, laughing as they described their escapades, thinking, "Oh my God, we're getting divorced and we're acting like a happy family." And finally, it was Sunday, and Libby was on her way over to see us for the last time before we left.

Just before Libby arrived, Gail said, "I think I'm making a mistake." It felt like whiplash, but I wanted him to feel that way so badly that I went along with it. I figured that the wonderful family time we'd spent together had brought him to his senses.

Frankly, I was so relieved that I wasn't prepared to question him too closely. In retrospect, the conversation that took place in those few minutes was surreal. We started to talk about the changes we'd make to improve our living situation and our marriage. We discussed selling our house outside Red Oak and moving back into town. We'd downsize, and there wouldn't be as much upkeep for Gail—he always complained about mowing our lawn. Best of all, Gail could spend more time with me in Washington during the week. I fell easily into my typical enthusiastic spiel, talking again about how Gail could volunteer at Walter Reed, or find other activities to keep himself busy while I was working.

He grimaced, and reiterated, "One thing I won't do. I will not participate in the Senate spouses' stuff, or anything else with your friends"—by which he meant the women I knew in Washington. I agreed. It was a small price to pay, and maybe I could eventually bring him around. I was entertaining a fantasy that everything would work out.

When Libby came over, we sat down with her to have a serious talk. Gail immediately started crying, which alarmed Libby. "Oh my God, what's going on?" she demanded.

I kept my cool. "Honey," I said, "Daddy and I have been having some problems and we need to reconnect and spend more time together."

"That's good," she said, her anxiety apparent. "You *should* spend more time together." We all took a deep breath, feeling that we had a positive way forward.

The weekend had been emotionally draining, but I felt a sense of hope as we began the drive back to Washington. Gail would be flying to Red Oak the following morning. On the drive, I carefully broached the subject of his affair.

"So, you won't be seeing her anymore?" I asked, not really thinking it was a question.

He turned to me with an agonized look. "You don't just stop loving someone," he said.

I guess that's when I knew, in my heart, that it wasn't going to work—that he hadn't changed his mind at all. All the fake plan-making was a diversion. He just hadn't wanted to tell Libby. I was right. Gail went back to Iowa and almost immediately filed for divorce.

He still resisted telling Libby. "She is too busy. We shouldn't be disturbing her." But I was done with the deception. It was time for the truth. I called her. "Libby, I need to tell you that your dad filed for divorce today. I know we said we were working on the relationship, but he made this decision on his own."

"Oh, Mom!"

"And there's more," I continued. "Your dad has been seeing another woman." I couldn't hold back a sob as I told her that, but Libby didn't cry. She kept saying, "I'm so sorry, I'm so sorry. Are you okay?" She was more worried about me than about her own feelings.

What I couldn't explain was the depth of the failure I felt. I knew so well from my own parents' divorce how crushing it was for a family, even when the kids are adults. You never again have that stable sense of history and unity. This was not the result I wanted. I would have gone to great lengths to protect my family. But I couldn't control Gail's choices, so I thought my job now was to be as supportive of Libby as I could.

She called him, of course, and she was angry. "How could you do this?" she demanded. He didn't have much of an answer except to tell her that she would have to accept his new relationship. "She will always be in my life," he said. "No ifs, ands, or buts."

So, the divorce went forward. To add insult to injury, he'd figured that I should pay him more than half of my take-home pay a month in alimony. Fortunately, the judge put an end to that.

We hadn't had a lot saved to begin with, and Gail had been paying for excursions with his girlfriend from our personal account. Also, before he filed for divorce, he'd gone into our accounts and taken almost everything, so I was literally living paycheck to paycheck for a while. When I was in Red Oak, I slept on my mom's couch until I found a place of my own. At least I knew I was better off than many women in a similar situation who don't have a job. I knew that I could save my paychecks and eventually get back on my feet. But for the time being, I felt pretty hopeless.

The clothes I'd managed to take were in a suitcase in my mom's computer room, and Gail made it difficult for me to retrieve my stuff from the house. When the judge initially ruled that I could stay in the house on certain weekends, Gail argued the point. Through it all, I was determined to get the whole thing over with, and as we prepared to go to court, there was one last sticking point—the shed where I kept my motorcycle. We both wanted the shed, and finally I let him have it. I didn't want to fight anymore.

My family and friends helped me pick up the pieces. Julie, Wade, and my friends showed up to help me move my furniture out of the house. Gail watched us with a holier-than-thou look on his face. One by one, we removed the pieces. I couldn't help noticing while I was gathering my belongings that all of his girlfriend's stuff was there—her perfume and her toiletries were in the bathroom before I had even moved out.

When we came to a certain picture, Gail put a firm hand down on it, stopping us.

"This one's mine," he said. "I bought it before we were married. It's staying with me."

I let him have it because it wasn't worth the fight. Julie didn't give up so easily. She had some fight left in her, and Gail sure knew how to push her buttons. Before we left, she said that she wanted to say good-bye and started heading back to the house. I knew that she was going to let him have it over that picture if I didn't stop her, so I called her back.

"It's not worth it, Julie," I said.

She bought the same picture for me later as a housewarming gift when I found a new place to live in Red Oak. It now hangs in my living room. A small victory.

Finally, it was over. Gail sold the house and made a nice profit. Then they packed up and moved to Florida. They were gone. And I didn't have to scan the parking lots when I went to the store to make sure they weren't there. I was glad it was over. But as I'm sure any divorced person can appreciate, the hard part was just beginning.

When the press stories came out about the divorce and the earlier abuse, I was horrified. I'd never meant for anybody to find out about the abuse. Gail was furious, of course, and he accused me of going to the press. The truth is, the only reason the whole thing came out was that the court records detailed the history of infidelity and abuse, and when Gail had filed, he'd neglected to have the records sealed. All it took was for a reporter from a small Des Moines paper to do a little digging—and the trouble in our marriage was exposed. It's impossible to describe how it feels to have the ugliest moments of your life laid bare for all to see. I was completely caught off guard.

I had never planned to share these details with anyone. As far as I was concerned, they would be locked away in the past. Although I had enormous respect for the #MeToo movement, and was proud of women who spoke out, I believe every person is different and deserves a choice about whether to speak or not. By failing to seal our court documents, Gail denied me that choice.

I was touring an Iowa hospital when reporters began peppering me with questions about my marriage and the abuse. They seemed to be looking at me with new eyes, and I had to remind them that I was the same person I had been the week before—but now they knew more about me. I felt very emotional about being publicly exposed, although some of my supporters reassured me that my very human drama made my fight for women victims of sexual assault and domestic violence seem more authentic. That was a comfort, but it was still hard to be the *story*, not just the advocate.

I relied heavily on my family and friends to get me through. My mom, my dad, and my siblings all rallied around me. But in re-creating my life I was on my own. It was really the first time as an adult that I'd be a single person, and I'd have to learn how to do that. I went through some of the stages many divorced people experience, growing closer to some friends and more distant from others—especially those who had known about Gail's affair and even socialized with him and his girlfriend behind my back.

My best friend from Red Oak, Dawn, and her husband, Brian, who own the local funeral chapel, had been our closest friends during our marriage. Dawn was always there for me completely, but when I told them about the divorce, I could tell that at first Brian was angry with me. I faced it head-on—I didn't want anything left unsaid. It turned out that Gail had convinced Brian I'd had an affair when I was deployed and that I was "dating" in Washington. Gail's version of events was that I'd betrayed him, and that's why he'd left me. Had I not felt so sickened, I would have laughed. If only people could see my life in Washington! I'd even tried to quell his paranoia by including my chief of staff in any meetings I had with men— a ridiculous double standard. As for having an affair during deployment, maybe Gail believed it, or maybe he was projecting. It hurt to have to defend myself against this accusation.

I told Brian, "Gail has been having an affair. None of what he said about me is true." Brian was upset about being deceived, and he was very apologetic. I realized that Gail didn't just want to leave me, he wanted to hurt me, and that was a hard lesson.

I heard the same story from other people, but slowly I began to find my community of support and reclaim my place. And I admit, as a public figure, I felt a sense of relief. I wouldn't have to make excuses for my inappropriate husband anymore! In particular, I didn't have to worry about Gail's Facebook postings, which were so embarrassing. Such as this one, which hurt me—a reposting of a joke: "What do you do if you see your ex-wife screaming and running bloody through your yard? [Answer] You shoot her again." I had a miserable flashback to things Gail used to say about his first wife, whom he hated—how he could have her killed and no one would ever know about it. I assumed he was just blowing off steam, but I chastised him for saying it. "Gail, you're talking about the mother of your girls." Gail had made his first wife the enemy, and now he was doing the same thing to me.

I felt that he had always tended to be misogynistic, which was ironic considering that he was married to a U.S. senator and had a daughter at West Point. In one of our last conversations, he called me a "feminazi"—a ridiculous, obsolete term. He was objecting to my support for the first female Rangers—my pride in their achievement. Of course, the Rangers was Gail's domain, and he couldn't stand to give the women credit. He didn't believe that they actually achieved it because they were worthy. He said, "No, they were just given a pass. There's so much attention on them. They allowed them to slide through and they got special treatment and training." That's the kind of mentality we don't want in the military.

"Those women made it on their own," I countered. It was so disheartening. "Would you want someone to say that about your daughter?" I asked. He had no response to that.

After the divorce, I felt the loss more than I care to admit. Again, it took Libby to snap me out of it. She needed a mom, and at times I felt more like a victim. I decided I couldn't let Gail rule my life. All survivors deal with their abuse in their own ways, and this was mine. I needed to stop thinking about it, talking about my ex-husband, and carry on for Libby. And that's what I did.

Protecting Libby became my number one concern. The one regret I have through all of it is not being a stronger mom for Libby. She understands now why I stayed with her father. I've explained to her that I did it for her stability. She didn't bat an eye. She sees the big picture and doesn't hold it against me. It's a regret that I have, though. I can't go back, so today I focus on moving on for her. I focus on not talking about him or wallowing in regret. But I now realize that I should have run from that marriage ten years earlier.

On my first day back in Washington after the story of my marriage was splashed all over the press, I was nervous about what I would encounter. My staff sat me down and briefed me: "Just ignore them when you're walking down the hall—you don't have to respond." During that first walk from my office, my stomach in knots, I encountered a gaggle of reporters at the bottom of the stairs. As I walked past, no one said a word. They stepped back as a group and several of them smiled at me, but there were no shouted questions. They quietly nodded their heads at me instead. This is not how things usually work with the press corps in Washington. I hadn't expected their reaction, and I can't express my gratitude enough for this compassionate press response.

In those early days, the media left me in peace. Those that did approach me were respectful, telling my staff, "If the senator wants to talk, we'd be happy to share her thoughts." They gave me space to decide when to speak out.

My colleagues were wonderfully supportive, including Democrats. Bernie Sanders and I are on opposite ends of the political spectrum, and we rarely speak. But to my surprise, one day he came up to me outside the Dirksen building and said, "I know we don't agree a lot, but what happened to you is absolutely wrong and I'm sorry for that." It was kind of him.

The president was also very supportive. I was sitting in a policy lunch when my phone buzzed and I saw it was President Trump's number. I stepped into the hallway and took the call. He said, "Melania just brought your situation to my attention. I wanted you to know that we love you and we're here for you. You're going to do great things." I was touched that he took the time to call, and his words comforted me.

I had private, very real doubts in that period. I didn't want to be a statistic. I didn't want to be that divorced person, or that abused woman. And I also worried that people would think less of me, or think me weak because I stayed with Gail after the abuse. But I'd just wanted my marriage to work. My experience gave me an even deeper understanding of the struggles women face in coping with abuse and assault. The fear and horror are complicated by the love or at least attachment they have for their abuser. I took the opportunity in those months after the divorce to do some real soul-searching about myself and my marriage. Although I had been shattered when Gail asked for a divorce, it hit me that for so much of my marriage I had been walking on eggshells.

Gail was a powerful, sometimes intimidating presence in our home. He was never wrong—you challenged him at your own risk. It was a form of emotional abuse that ultimately left me voiceless.

I learned to never argue back, to just shut up and go with what he wanted. It was easier to keep the peace. It was a constant in my marriage—his effort to control and put me down, to keep me in my place even as I was excelling in public life.

It wasn't healthy, but I didn't even realize how unhealthy it was. I buried myself in my work and in raising Libby, and hoped things would improve with time. I constantly made excuses for Gail in my own mind, without examining my needs or status in the marriage. Gail thought nothing of lying to our friends about my having affairs, but there I was always trying to protect his reputation. I thought that was love.

From a practical standpoint, I was worried about moving into the next election cycle with this big revelation hanging over my head. I could see the headline in my mind: "Joni Ernst, who espouses Christian values, is now a divorced woman. She couldn't make it work." I had that worry. But my fear never materialized. My Christian supporters were very understanding. After all, none of us are perfect. There was very little blowback, and I began to realize that my experience had a universal resonance to it. Other people have suffered domestic violence and rape. Others have gone through divorce. I wasn't alone.

I found that there was something liberating about facing the demons in my past. Once it was out in the open, I decided that embracing what happened to me in my life and talking about it— the rape, the physical and emotional abuse, and the divorce—could help other women who were suffering in silence. I wanted them to know that they weren't alone, and nobody is immune, even a United States senator. Despite many offers from journalists wanting to do an exclusive on my story, I decided to give it to Bloomberg's Jennifer Jacobs. I had known Jennifer since I served in the Iowa state senate, when she was a reporter for the *Des Moines Register*, covering the

Iowa state legislature. I trusted her and I knew she would tell my story with compassion and grace.

I was particularly intent on sending the message that women should not be ashamed. Shame was a big hurdle for me to overcome. I remember thinking, "How can I face the public with this shame?" I had to take back my personal dignity, and talking about it helped me do that. Anyone who knows me knows I'm not a person who easily shares her private life. I was raised not to talk about personal business. But in this case, I decided it was important enough to take the risk of being open. And I was rewarded by an outpouring of support and sisterhood.

Once my story was fully out in the open, in my own words, many women reached out to me. I was overwhelmed by their kindness and by the ways they reminded me of my own strength. They'd say, "You're a lieutenant colonel, you're a senator, and you've gone through a rape experience and you've moved on. You've gone through domestic abuse and you've moved on. You've gone through your husband's infidelity and divorce, and you've moved on." They told me they were inspired that I could go through so much while continuing to be a strong leader.

Out on the road in Iowa, women would come up to me at events and give me a hug. Sometimes they'd just say, "Joni, I understand." And as scarred as I was, I was glad to be able to say back to them, "I understand you, too."

Chapter Eleven

WHY WE SERVE

"Welcome back, ma'am."

Driving through Camp Arifjan in Kuwait with a congressional delegation before Thanksgiving 2019, I was warmly greeted as a returning veteran and a friend. It was a great feeling! At first, the camp looked completely unfamiliar, and it took a while for me to get my bearings. So much had changed since I'd been stationed there in 2003–2004. I didn't quite know where I was until we drove by the Army Central Command Headquarters. Next to it I recognized rows of warehouses, now used for supplies. In my day, during deployment, they were housing units with bunk beds stacked high.

Today, the character of the camp is different, with the thousands of soldiers who had deployed to Iraq a decade and a half ago replaced by a smaller military presence, along with civilian contractors and third-country nationals.

We call these congressional delegations "CODELs" for short, and the purpose of this one was to visit Kuwait and Afghanistan to explore with military and political leaders in those countries how we are progressing in the national security space to make sure that our country is safe.

All three senators on the CODEL were women—me, Kirsten

Gillibrand, and Shelley Moore Capito. We were joined by three male House members—Jason Smith of Missouri, John Curtis of Utah, and Mike Turner of Ohio. Two of them, Curtis and Smith, had never been to Afghanistan before. We represented different committees of jurisdiction—Armed Services, Foreign Intelligence, Appropriations, and Ways and Means. All of these committees have an interest in what's going on in the region.

Our male congressmen joked about the male-female breakdown, openly noting that all the women came from the Senate and all of the men came from the lower body, the House, but everyone was pleased that the CODEL was bipartisan; even some of the military leaders mentioned that many times CODELs are all Republicans or all Democrats. I noted that once again the women of the Senate were choosing to be bipartisan.

My greatest pleasure came from visiting Iowans from the Des Moines–based 103rd Sustainment Command of the Army Reserves, which is stationed in Kuwait to support the fight against ISIS and our continuing operations. They welcomed me heartily, very happy to see a face from home. These reserve troops, under the command of General John Sullivan, are the often-forgotten heroes of our engagement. Several of them mentioned to me that they sometimes hear people say, "I didn't know we were still over there." Yes, indeed, they are, and these troops take their mission very seriously. They work extremely hard. It's a difficult mission, yet overall morale is incredible. Since we were visiting the week before Thanksgiving, they described the months-long planning that the 103rd had undertaken to feed troops a Thanksgiving dinner they could remember. I assured them that this was a valuable endeavor. When the entire nation is celebrating Thanksgiving back home, you definitely want to feel a part of the celebration when you are so far away. I remember that vividly from my own service.

I also heard about an intensive ruck march planned for early December. This is known as the Norwegian Foot March Challenge, which has its origins over a hundred years ago, and which our soldiers can adopt to earn a special badge. The challenge involves marching thirty kilometers (about eighteen and a half miles) carrying 25-pound rucksacks—a physical endeavor that requires plenty of conditioning and grit. I told them wistfully that I would have loved to join them, and I meant it. I love ruck marches, as I've said. With the broiling heat giving way to a cooler climate in December, it was the perfect time for the march.

After Camp Arifjan, we flew to Kabul, Afghanistan, where the discussions turned to a sober evaluation of whether we are doing enough in the region to keep the terrorists at bay and stop our homeland from being targeted. Much of the conversation centered on the Taliban and ISIS.

Frankly, it can be hard to feel optimistic in Afghanistan. Scenes of tribal warfare are discouraging, and political stability is elusive, with a contentious election recount going on as we visited. In the provinces, terrorist-based organizations hold tremendous power over the population. U.S. peace talks with the Taliban have been off and on, but are ongoing. (Three weeks after our visit, a car bomb at Bagram Air Base would once again complicate negotiations.)

Americans don't always appreciate the importance of these fact-finding missions. I've heard some bad-mouthing over the years, as if they're frivolous expenses with no real purpose. That couldn't be further from the truth. It's essential that Congress gets to experience the real picture on the ground. In Washington, we receive high-level briefings from generals and admirals all the time. But to actually go into a country where we're engaged and be able to talk with the soldiers is valuable, and it's also an uplifting experience.

Shelley, Kirsten, and I talked to young women who were American soldiers there. One young infantryman, in her early twenties, was only the third woman to receive the combat infantryman's badge. She mentioned that she'd recently been in a six-hour firefight.

For me, these conversations were a mental trip back to when I was in the Middle East in my role as a commander. So much has changed for women since I commanded a transportation unit, and women were just sprinkled across the ranks. It was 2013 before women could formally serve in combat fields or occupation units. Now these brave women are stepping up with ease.

Let me tell you, they're tough! They are physically strong, and they have to be mentally strong, too, to endure the harsh conditions and the intense and lengthy battles. It takes intestinal fortitude to keep driving on. Those who still worry that women are too weak for combat, and that their presence might hold back the males, should meet these women.

One young woman was being promoted to first lieutenant and when she found out I'd be visiting, she asked her commander if I could promote her. I was thrilled and honored. It was a high point of the trip for me to stand up for this patriotic young woman. I thought back to when I was a lieutenant with my whole life ahead of me. Like me, she was filled with optimism for the future, and she gave a very moving speech about the opportunity to serve her country. I noted that almost twenty-five years earlier, I had been promoted from second to first lieutenant by the commander of the 75th Ranger Regiment, Colonel Bill Leszczynski, at Fort Benning, Georgia, and was surrounded in my promotion ceremony by the predecessors of these young men and women.

My own daughter has told me that she's considering entering combat arms and fully pursuing a career in the military. I recalled an event in Iowa when I was privileged to meet General Jennifer Walter, the first female Iowa Air Guard general in the Iowa National Guard.

She spoke about the limited options that were presented to her when she graduated from high school in 1974 and wanted to join the military. She could have a clerking job or be a typist or a nurse. But she didn't accept those limitations. She forged her own path, and today has become a role model for women who seek military careers. So, times are changing, and many of us wish they'd change faster.

Leaving Afghanistan, I felt better than I had before going on the trip. One reason was hearing from senior American military leaders how the Afghanistan officers, who had been educated in a more Soviet era and style of leadership and fighting, have retired and moved on, and now there is a whole new group of up-and-coming Afghanistan service members that are educated in more of a Western or democratic way of thinking and decision making. And they can actually make decisions on their own now. Visiting Camp Morehead, which is the commando training center outside Kabul, I was impressed by the training programs for Afghan commandoes, including women soldiers, under the direction of NATO's Resolute Support Mission.

They still have a long way to go, and ultimately the solution in Afghanistan won't be military but political, involving governance. Our armed services are part of that solution, as is our State Department and our partner nations.

The trip had a restorative quality for all of us. It felt good to get out of Washington and be with our constituents overseas. It's easy for some to lose perspective in Washington, and being in Afghanistan reminded us in a very tangible way of what our service means. A lot of lives and treasure have been expended in this fight, and the terrorist organizations have a tenacious hold. But gradually we're working our way to more of a maintenance project where we have a smaller number of troops whose role is to advise and assist Afghan Special Forces and the Afghan Army. At some point, they will be able to operate on their own, but right now they still need our support. They're getting stronger and better equipped. It's just taking a lot longer than we'd hoped.

One evening we got together with constituents, and I sat down at a round table with some of the civilian contractors from my state. A young man serving as a security contractor asked me, "Does the American public even know what's going on over here?" Everyone at the table leaned forward with intense interest. It was something they all wanted to know.

"Truthfully, no," I said with regret.

He grimaced. "Thank you for being honest."

I empathized. How difficult it must be for these men and women to be inside Afghanistan and feel that no one at home is listening. I assured them that I and my colleagues were committed to bringing their stories back, and shining a spotlight on the work they were doing.

Many security contractors start out in the military and then choose to return once their enlistments are up to provide security for various officials. Some of them have been there for many years. And even though they occasionally get time off to come back to the States, this is their life now. As one soldier put it, it hurts to feel "emotionally abandoned" by Americans who don't understand the contribution they're making.

It's a sad reality that people's attention spans aren't that great. Our engagement has been lengthy, and only a small percentage of Americans are serving there. Most families and communities aren't affected at all. They can go about their days without ever thinking about Afghanistan. It's human nature to move on to other concerns when you're not personally affected. But we, as elected officials, have to find ways to keep those serving in lonely parts of the world in the public mind. That starts with our CODELs to Afghanistan. It means so much to those young men and women to see us there. And when we get back home, we'll talk about them, share their insights, and show their photos—bringing their service to life for our constituents.

After Afghanistan, we overnighted in Brussels for crew rest. During our stopover, we were hosted by Ambassador Kay Bailey Hutchison, our permanent representative to NATO.

Kay is always an inspiration. Her energy, commitment and, yes, grit, are impressive. We admire her twenty-year career in the Senate, as the first female senator from Texas, where she served on the Armed Services Committee. In 2017, five years after she retired from the Senate, Kay was appointed by President Trump to represent us at NATO. Over dinner, she talked about the importance of her work in Brussels; it was a week before the leaders' summit. Kay feels strongly that we're not just members of NATO; we're *leaders* of NATO. No one understands being a leader better than Kay.

Flying back to Washington from Brussels, early Thanksgiving week, we were tired but invigorated. For me, it was the complete absence of rhetoric, which pervades D.C. Instead, we had been flooded with reality and inspiration.

Both would be needed during the upcoming election season. Back in June, as I did every year, I donned jeans, boots, and a leather jacket and jumped on my Harley to lead hundreds of motorcyclists in my annual Roast and Ride fund-raising event. We rode from the Big Barn Harley-Davidson in Des Moines to the central Iowa town of Boone, for a big family-friendly hog roast. In 2019, with Democratic presidential candidates flooding the state, there was a lot of public attention on the 2020 election, and it would be a reelection year for me, too. At the Roast and Ride, as my fellow Iowans chowed down on barbecue, I announced my candidacy for reelection, surrounded by my staunchest supporters, Senator Grassley and Governor Kim

Reynolds. Nikki Haley, former governor of South Carolina and ambassador to the United Nations, joined us as a keynote speaker. It was heartening to hear from so many supporters about how inspiring the image of Kim, Nikki, and I standing together on that stage was to them.

It was early days, with nearly a year and a half before the election, but the modern realities of campaigning have turned election periods into lengthy marathons. My announcement was a way of putting a stake in the ground, of claiming my place and speaking about my vision.

In spite of all the media, it can be hard to get people's attention these days. I notice when I'm speaking at events, a lot of them are so busy filming me on their phones that I'm not sure they're actually hearing what I have to say. At an event one day with Vice President Pence in Des Moines, we were running about a half an hour late, and I was worried people would be unhappy. I *hate* to be late! To make matters worse, they'd had everyone leave their phones outside the room, so they didn't have them to help pass the time. When we arrived, I asked my state director, Clarke Scanlon, and my campaign manager, Sam Pritchard, "Are they upset we're late?" They laughed. "Oh, no," they said. "Everyone's having a good time. Since they don't have their phones, they're actually talking to each other."

As I write this, the campaign season is in full swing, and we're all aware of how much is at stake. The 2020 election is a referendum on my party, and in a presidential election year, much of the focus is on the national contest. It will be a particularly fierce partisan year, exacerbated by the impeachment trial. Several Democrats have declared their intention to run against me, with some in the media calling me "vulnerable"—a designation I mostly ignore. I'm going to keep doing what I do. With the primary season extending into the summer of 2020, it will be a while before I have an actual opponent. (I admit that I was disappointed when Kirsten Gillebrand endorsed one of my potential opponents early in the primary season without telling me. It was hurtful and it made me sad because I felt like we had a better relationship than that—just a heads-up would have been enough for me to understand that national politics sometimes dictates that we don't always play nice. Today, we are still friends, and I understand that politics can be messy, but it felt like a true lesson that Washington is a much different place than Iowa.)

Even in the early days, there are signs that the campaign against me is going to be ugly. Eddie Mauro, a Democratic businessman running in the primary, produced an ad attacking me on guns. He took footage from my 2014 shooting range ad and doctored it to make it appear that I was shooting at him as he walked through a field. The bullets from "my" gun barely missed him.

It was disgusting. I didn't even know the guy, and he was posting video of me shooting at him as if I were some old country gunslinger. On guns, my opponents think they can simply label me as a "gun nut" and try to make it look as if I support violence. It's a fear tactic I've seen time and again from the left. Yes, I've been open that I support the rights of law-abiding citizens to exercise their Second Amendment rights. For me, it's not just a commitment to constitutional rights, but also a practical matter I learned as a girl raised on a farm in a rural area. Guns are simply a part of life for many families across America that use them for everything from self-protection to hunting and recreation.

One woman from New York City said to me at an event, "I don't understand why people even need guns at all." I told her that if she lived in a rural area she might feel differently. Before Gail and I divorced, we lived out in the country north of Red Oak. It was isolated, and maybe we had one or two deputies on duty for the whole area, and their response time to a 911 call was at least thirty minutes.

"In New York, you have police officers on every block," I said. "In rural areas, people feel as if they need a greater level of protection because we might have to fend for ourselves." I share these rural insights with those who have knee-jerk reactions when the topic of guns comes up.

I try not to get bogged down by the horse race. Soon I will begin my ninety-nine-county tour for 2020, which is separate from campaigning. It isn't always easy, because it seems as if we're in the midst of one great public conversation, much of it directed at international issues. I have strongly stated that North Korea and Russia are not our friends—and that Ukraine is. Of course, I have a special feeling for Ukraine because it was such an important part of my personal awakening. (I'd had the opportunity to spend time with the ambassador on my CODEL to the Ukraine earlier in 2019. She was a lovely host, and she gave me a "F*CK Putin" coffee mug as a keepsake.)

However, my reelection campaign will be focused on the homeland, talking about the issues that are closest to Iowans' hearts. My mantra, whether I'm on the trail or performing my Senate duties, is to always put Iowa and Iowans first. There's a very different quality to running for reelection. My first campaign was aspirational, but now I have a track record. Now I have to show what I've accomplished and how I plan to build on it in a second term.

I'm proud of my record on behalf of Iowa farmers. I've fought for them on the Farm Bill and I've been relentless on biofuels, even when it means challenging the president. I do more than talk. I've actually stepped up and done something about it, and achieved some legislative success.

But Iowans don't really want to hear a laundry list of achievements. They'll say, "That's good, but what are you going to do in the next six years?" Part of my vision is helping farmers chart a course for agriculture that fully embraces new technologies. Looking ahead, so much of what we do will be precision agriculture and focusing on conservation. Without reverting to labels or calling themselves "greenies," Iowa farmers—especially the younger ones—are very engaged in advances in soil health and clean water technologies. These are issues I am committed to as well.

For the last couple of decades, our farmers have been amazing conservationists. I visited one farmer with a cattle feedlot who boasted proudly that the water coming out of his containment area was actually cleaner than the water in the creek, by EPA standards. I always say that our farmers are our first conservationists. They're the ones whose lives depend on the land, and they want healthy soil and healthy water. They're the ones who will take care of that land. We may not be in favor of a big bureaucracy like the Green New Deal, which would devastate our economy, but we're working every day on solutions.

When they ask me what I bring to the table, I can point to legislative efforts involving conservation. And I always highlight the bipartisan nature of our efforts, because advancing new technologies is not strictly a Republican or Democratic effort. For example, my Democratic colleague Michigan senator Debbie Stabenow and I worked together on the conservation section of the last farm bill, and we'll continue to do that.

The technology of the future belongs to all of us. In the past, many of the heartland areas have been left behind, and I'm determined to change that. I'm a cofounder of the GPS Caucus, along with Democratic senator Tammy Duckworth of Illinois, Representative Dave Loebsack, a Democrat from Iowa, and Republican representative Don Bacon of Nebraska. The Global Positioning System has many applications, but we're particularly interested in its use for precision agriculture and enhanced emergency services—not to mention the way it supports a vast ag economy that will improve lives and create jobs in the heartland. Those are the practical and visionary initiatives I'll be talking about on the campaign trail.

To get these messages across to the public means being accessible. But accessibility is also about listening to the people in the state. My best ideas come from them. I find that when I'm doing business visits or farm visits, the partisan labels easily fall away in the face of our shared interests. People are really proud of their work and they want to show it off. They want me to take their success stories and their ambitions back to Washington. They're especially eager to show me their inventive solutions in robotics and software—such as an amazing new milking machine I saw recently that's a fine and effective example of artificial intelligence on the farm.

In Iowa, we're always very close to the land. We're small enough that even our big towns or cities are still pretty rural. Des Moines has around 300,000 people. You drive five minutes out of Des Moines and you're in farm country. You see a field and you see a farmer planting in his field. There's a connection. Most of the innovation in our cities and universities is connected to agriculture. At the same time, much of our manufacturing is in rural areas. I like to say that there's no real urban-versus-rural divide in Iowa. We're all supporting one another's endeavors.

I am a servant of my constituents. While I'm grappling with the big picture, I'm also taking care of people in their day-to-day lives. Legislation is a long road, so my staff is constantly asking what we can do to help people in the moment. We pride ourselves on responding to every call, and I'm proud to have such great caseworkers out in the state. Even if someone calls the office with a problem that needs to get resolved by another agency on the state or local level, my staffers will walk them through it and connect them with the right resource. It's the neighborly way. We never say, "Sorry, that's someone else's department." Our mantra is to care and serve, and sometimes that's difficult—people call us because they're struggling and upset and they're not always polite about it. But that's okay. It comes with the territory. They don't always love you on the front lines, but you can still help them.

Looking ahead, I'll have a lot of juggling to do to perform my duties and also campaign for reelection. One of the duties that most senators collectively dread is fund-raising. I can assure you, absolutely no elected official relishes those fund-raising calls! Even though I have a higher profile now than I did when I first ran for the Senate, it's sometimes not that different than when I was sitting in my attic, listening to people on the other end of the line asking, "Who are you, again?" It's grueling.

As I plan for a season of campaigning, I have to take a deep breath and think harder than ever about time management. I have to figure out how to be fully present in both my job and the campaign without burning out. What can I do to renew my energy when I'm flagging? Usually, that renewal involves time with Libby. I think most mothers can understand that.

I'm only human, and while I wish I could go 24/7, I know I can't. I've experienced in the past reaching my limit because I haven't rested properly, and I've hit that wall that everyone hits when they're pushed too hard—even senators. I've had the feeling of waking up in yet another hotel room and wondering, "Where am I?"

When I start feeling overwhelmed or burned out, I look to my heroes—often women in public service who achieved seemingly impossible feats. One of these is Margaret Chase Smith, who was elected to the Senate from Maine in 1948. When she began serving, not only was she was the only woman senator, but she'd already served in the House for almost eight years. She went on to serve twenty-four years, and during that time she even ran for president in 1964. Smith once spoke of her creed of public service: "It must be a complete dedication to the people and to the nation with full recognition that every human being is entitled to courtesy and consideration, that constructive criticism is not only to be expected but sought, that smears are not only to be expected but fought, that honor is to be earned but not bought." Whenever I experience exhaustion or doubts, I think of Smith, bravely setting the highest goals for herself and fulfilling them, at a time when women had barely started to make themselves heard in the public sphere. A crusty Mainer, she didn't have much tolerance for self-pity or complaining. For her, service was a high honor, a necessity, and the payment of a debt owed for the privilege of being American. When I look for renewed energy to serve, I know that I stand on the shoulders of unstoppable women like Smith.

Chapter Twelve

GIVING THANKS

A light snow is falling as I pull into the driveway of my small house in Red Oak. It's a late Friday evening in January 2020, and I've just flown in from Washington, with a full weekend of activities ahead of me. I go inside and turn up the thermostat, put away the groceries I picked up on the way from the airport in Omaha, and start fixing dinner.

A silence hangs over Red Oak at night—so unlike my FOB in D.C. It helps me decompress, but to be honest, I'm still not used to coming home to an empty house, without my daughter and husband to greet me. Being single for the first time in my adult life is a little bit like having a limb cut off. I find it hard to maneuver. Even though I am surrounded by staff, colleagues, and constituents for most of my waking moments, I get lonely sometimes. I especially miss having someone to talk to at night. Even when my marriage was going through hard times, I could always talk to Gail at the end of the day. But truthfully, it's been a long time since I've had anyone to tell about my life who really understood my challenges and frustrations. So, I'm actually missing something that didn't really exist before my divorce—somebody who understands my need to be out on the road in Iowa, or in Washington. Somebody who accepts me and all the pieces of my life. I guess being alone brings that need into focus. I hope someday I'll have that kind of partner, but I'm not ready to think about it now. I'm trying to get used to being on my own. On a rare day off, I tinker, mowing the small patch of grass in front and painting the old mud room. My backyard deck and narrow yard are still a work in progress.

When I go out with friends, mostly couples, I can feel like a third wheel, even though I know how much they love me. When I'm having dinner with Mom, the thought will flash through my mind, "Here we are, two divorced women." It's not what I would ever have expected. But at those times when I'm tempted to feel sorry for myself, I'm pulled back in to a sense of gratitude for all the loving support I've received, not just from family and friends, but from my colleagues, too. The women senators have been like a rock to me, and others, like my dearest champion, Senator Grassley, have promised to pray for me—and mean it. I always think of the words of Iowa native Abigail Van Buren ("Dear Abby"): "If you want a place in the sun, you have got to put up with a few blisters."

I aspire to live a life of gratitude, to avoid feeling anger or despair about my relatively small problems. In the same way, I often reflect on what it means to approach public service with gratitude. Sometimes it can be hard to remember just how lucky we are to be Americans and live in this country. Our public discourse is antagonistic these days, and the noise of debate often masks our deeper unity. "Our shared values define us more than our differences," the late Senator McCain liked to say. He lived that dictate in his service, and for this we all miss his steady presence.

Recently I was moderating an event for former U.S. ambassador Nikki Haley at George Washington University. She was promoting her book, *With All Due Respect*. During Nikki's time as ambassador she traveled all over the world, often to countries that were very violent and torn apart by tribal warfare. The women in one village described to her how invaders had come in, taken their babies, thrown them into a fire, and then forced the women to eat the burnt flesh of their children. When Nikki told this story, the audience gasped in horror. It seemed unimaginable.

When we hear these stories, we hold tight to our great good fortune as Americans. That good fortune transcends party disputes, or even who is president. We have the freedom to vote for whichever candidate we choose, and when people say they're going to move to another country because they disagree with the president, it feels like a betrayal of our principles—and, by the way, few of the people who make that threat actually *do* move, which proves the point that in their hearts they don't want to live anywhere else.

When I read my Twitter feed, it can sometimes put me on my heels. The ugliness of the comments is stunning. I can't post an innocuous item about visiting an Iowa business or meeting with a community group without it generating a slew of messages, attacking me for everything from my looks to my beliefs. They seem to be saying, "How dare you exist?"

I often hear the excuse, "People are angry," but let's think about that. I understand that some people are struggling. But I was brought up knowing the value of tenacity, and a drive to figure out ways to solve problems. If you're on a farm and the tractor goes on the blink, what good is anger? What good is anger when your husband is in the hospital and you still have to do harvest? How is anger helpful when a storm destroys your crops? Even when the threat is government policies, like tariffs, or decisions that hamstring production, anger doesn't get you very far.

I think many Iowans relate to this. We have a certain can-do spirit. For the most part I find that no one wants to sit around and gripe, much less spew vitriol on Twitter. People want to get things done. So, when I'm in Iowa, the overarching feeling I get from every-day people that I meet is a sense that they're able to shut out the noise, live their lives, and focus on their families, instead of being constantly outraged and upset.

They have a simple quest—to make their circumstances bet-ter and improve their communities. Iowa is the land of continu-ous improvement, not the land of "woe is me." It's the way we were raised. And when times are harsh, we try to figure out together what we can do to get through.

It's only through gratitude that I have been able to challenge myself and achieve what I have today. My gratitude for my home-town, love for my family, and appreciation for the men and women fighting in our armed forces are all things that drive me. And smaller things, too. Mothers caring for their daughters. Neighbors refusing to let their communities struggle. The core of all of the bills that I vote to pass comes out of my thanks for these people and the desire to help them. My votes give back to these communities that, while overworked and underserved, strain vigorously to lift themselves up. Without special people like that, what we're doing in the U.S. Senate would have no point.

Seeing the way my life has turned out so far, the one constant has been being true to myself. From the farm to the military to the government, I've learned to outwork everybody else, to push myself physically and mentally, to brush myself off when I fall down, to listen more than I speak, to prefer collaboration to conflict, to have the courage to make unpopular decisions, and to always live by the Golden Rule—to treat others as I would want to be treated, and to represent others as I would want to be represented.

We are what and whom we love. That's where all of our work and energies begin. In my life, I've been a part of vast enterprises—the military and government. My circle of love is wide, including my family, my friends, the men and women in my military family, my beloved Iowa neighbors, my congregation, my colleagues, and all the people who step up to partner with me in doing my work. I'm blessed to be surrounded by so much love and support, even in the hardest times. My family, while not that expressive about our feelings, holds strong when we need each other the most. Our appreciation for each other and the little (and sometimes big) courtesies we do for each other help me keep my head on straight. It's the same in my work. You can have an army of smart, capable people, but if they're not bonded in a shared mission, you don't have an army at all—you have a bunch of individuals working for their own purposes.

Despite the hurt and abuse I endured from my ex-husband, I can be thankful for the struggle, which has only made me a stronger leader and a better advocate for women. I believe in the power of women and the strength we all have to become the best leaders we can be whether through service, profession, or family. As I look ahead and prepare to run for my second term in office, I am filled with gratitude for the opportunity to serve and to lead. I know how privileged I am, and I'm humbled by the honor.

Living in love is never easy; we stumble along the way. The Bible tells us, no matter what, to rely on God's love for us. And that's the way I live my life, even when my relationships fracture.

On Sunday mornings in Iowa, the mighty bell chimes from the historic old Mamrelund Lutheran Church in Stanton, where I've worshipped ever since childhood. Sitting in a pew next to my mother, I reflect, as I often do, on the special American spirit of this house of worship. When it was founded 150 years ago, the mission of Mamrelund was to be a haven to all the new immigrants from Sweden who came to our country to live in its promise. Since that time, its doors have remained open to newcomers—an invitation to community.

Looking around, I see the community of the faithful, my neighbors who have been there through every stage of my life. They pause here to pray and give thanks before returning to a world where they will struggle to coax abundance from the fields, surviving through seasons of drought and floods and hundred-year storms, from economic blights and the actions of leaders who don't have their interests at heart. They place their faith in God, as they always have.

We rise to sing.

Now thank we all our God, with heart and hands and voices,
Who wondrous things has done, in Whom this world rejoices;
Who from our mothers' arms has blessed us on our way
With countless gifts of love, and still is ours today.

I reflect on those words as I sing them. The "countless gifts" are all around us—and so I renew my vow to start each day with gratitude in my heart and the grace to keep moving forward.

Acknowledgments

Growing up in Iowa, I learned the power of community, and that lesson carried through during my time in the military and in public office. None of us is alone, and our achievements are the result of the efforts of others. Like all of my endeavors, writing this book has been a collaborative process, inspired and aided by many people.

Steve Troha, my literary agent at Folio Literary Management, was the first person to encourage me to write my heartland story. From the start, Steve recognized that my story was not just about me but was an ode to the special character of Iowa. Steve introduced me to Catherine Whitney, who became my collaborator and friend, and helped me tell the story with authenticity and passion. Natasha Simons, my editor at Simon & Schuster, was excited about this book from the start, and she has skillfully guided its creation. I'm so grateful to have such a strong team behind me.

Every day I appreciate the dedication and support of my Senate staff, who work tirelessly from early morning until late at night to serve Iowans and the nation—under the strong leadership of Lisa Goeas, my chief of staff, and Clarke Scanlon, my state director. The Senate can feel like a whirlwind, but they are remarkably steady through the ups and downs of legislating, and my staff never loses sight of the purpose of our work—to fully represent the people of Iowa and serve the national good. I can't thank them enough for all they do.

In twenty-three years in the military, I was blessed to be part of a community whose character, bravery, and collegiality changed my life. Even though I retired from the National Guard in 2015, I continue to be connected to this community, which remains a part of me. I will always hold the men and women of the 1168th Transportation Company and the 185th Combat Sustainment Support Battalion in my heart.

I want to give special thanks to the colleagues and friends who have stood by me through struggles and success, and whose example has taught me what it means to be selfless. In particular, I am grateful to Senator Chuck Grassley, my mentor, my model, and my friend. Chuck is a constant example of what it means to serve. And many thanks to Iowa governor Kim Reynolds, who has been a good friend, colleague, and a constant example of leadership.

I could not do what I do without my friends—Brian, Dawn, and Joshua LeRette; Budd and Sandy Krcilek; the Benskin Girls, Deb, Barb, and Cheryl, and their families; Mike Luna; Dave Trotter; Owen Lawler and many more in my Montgomery County, Iowa, family.

My family sustains me, lifts me up, and makes sacrifices for me. My parents, Dick and Marilyn Culver, instilled in me the values I still live today, and taught me I could do anything I set out to do. I am lucky to have such a supportive family—my sister, Julie, and her husband, Joe Herbert; my brother, Wade, and his wife, Sarah; and my stepmom, Monica. My daughter, Libby, gives me great joy. I am so proud of the fine young woman she has become.

Finally, I am grateful every day for the people of Iowa, whose stamina and daily practice of love and service keep me grounded and inspire me to live a life of service. I am proud to be their senator.